JUMP START!

*Go from New Manager to Making a
Difference in Your First 90 Days*

2ND EDITION

ISBN: 1492229911
ISBN 13: 9781492229919

TABLE OF CONTENTS

PREFACE
My Story

First a confession: I never wanted to be a manager.

Scout's honor.

Growing up, and all the way through my first few years of my first job, I never wanted to be a manager. Hell, I didn't even want to be in the business world.

I wanted to be an astronaut.

Not just any astronaut, mind you. The first man to walk on Mars. Big-time stuff. The plan had one flaw: bad eyesight, bad enough that NASA wanted nothing to do with me.

But the technology bug had bitten me, so soon I was heading off to my first job after getting my degree in Mathematics and Computer Science from the University of Wisconsin-Stevens Point. I was a software developer full of ideas. Even though I knew I wasn't going to go down in history for walking on another planet, I was enthusiastic and ready to write some rockin' software and achieve something that mattered.

It didn't turn out that way; I ran into my first bad boss and a corporate culture that was very, very foreign to me. All I had ever known was the academic world, where for the students it was as close to a true meritocracy as you can get in this imperfect world. It was all clear: do good, get an "A", do bad, get a "D" (or worse). In the best classes, ideas were king; the better the idea the more likely you were to get heard. And people wanted to hear; we all were looking for that great idea. In my new corporate job, I was stunned by the utter drudgery of it all. I couldn't see any drive to create something special, no bias for hearing and implementing the next good idea. I found little passion and no "juice". All the ideas seemed to have to come down from on high, and I was just the rookie. It was a world that made no sense to me, and I couldn't understand why anyone in the world would choose to stay in a situation like this. I wondered what in the world I had stepped into.

That all changed for me when I got the chance to take an in-house management training class. I saw an opening, a way to change things. If I could get to be a manager, even a team leader, I could create a team environment that had some meaning, and maybe get rid of the drudgery on the way to making a difference.

With that in mind, I set out on my management journey. I took my cues from the sports world, wondering why the kind of camaraderie, passion, and drive for excellence I saw every weekend on television never seemed to show up in my corner of the business world. I felt deep down that the fire and the enthusiasm of a sports team should be able to be replicated in a business setting, and couldn't seem to figure out why I never seemed to see it. If I could bring that spirit and culture to my teams, I thought that doing something that mattered would follow along.

I thought it would be (relatively) easy. I figured I'd run into some people on my teams that had no interest in what I was trying to do and would be a challenge, but I figured it was such a better way to work that they'd eventually see it my way. But what I hadn't figured on was the issues I kept having with management above me and the culture of the organizations I was in. I hadn't figured on the persistent negativity, the persistent attitude of regarding workers as mere tools, and the persistent focus on results at the expense of humanity, rather than humanity driving results.

Over the intervening years I kept up the fight as I built, rebuilt, and revitalized organizations of various shapes and sizes. I always could show improvement, sometimes dramatic improvement in these organizations, but I was almost always seemingly operating outside the lines. I was committed to finding a way to make the work important, to give it some juice, to build up the staff, to help them discover their potential, and to achieve something that mattered.

I didn't get it. How could I be the only manager this seemed to make sense to?

One day I realized it wasn't me; it's the management systems that have evolved over the last fifty years. They've become obsolete and dangerous; the damage they've inflicted (and continued to inflict) has to end. My own daughters are now beginning their work careers, and there's no way I want them to have to put up with the kinds of people-hostile environments I did. I can't be satisfied with fixing organizations one at a time anymore; it's too slow. It's time for a bigger answer.

The way new leaders get trained (or don't get trained, more frequently) is not working. You may be a brand-new leader who finds yourself in your first leadership role but no real idea of how to make the shift from individual contributor to leader. Or you may be a more experienced leader who has just been given a new group to work with and aren't quite sure how to take charge in a way that is quick and effective without having to stumble and fumble your way to the answers.

In either case, you need to get some practical, real-world information that works. Now. Which is what this book is all about.

Jump Start! Is the first step in a series that is intended to provide the insight, information, and practical training for a whole new way of leading: High Voltage Leadership. The whole idea behind High Voltage Leadership is to get leaders up to speed quickly with tools and tactics that work, and work quickly in a way that maximizes team performance now and gong forward. It sets you up to make a difference in a hurry so you can get noticed.

More on this later, but if you just gotta hear more check out the home of High Voltage Leadership: www.RedstoneServicesLLC.us.

It's time for a "new generation" of leaders, a new way to lead. The old ways of managing need to be relegated to the scrap heap of history; it's a big job and we need to get at it. Read on; then come join us!

SECTION 1:

GET READY

CHAPTER 1

WHY WE ABSOLUTELY NEED YOU NOW

People say to me, "You were a roaring success. How did you do it?" I go back to what my parents taught me. Apply yourself. Get all the education you can, but then, by God, do something. Don't just stand there, make something happen.

— Lee Iacocca

Welcome To Your (New) World

So you're a newly-minted manager, taking charge of people, processes, or an operational group for the first time in your life. Congratulations! Since you've found out about your new role I'm sure you've been on a roller-coaster emotional ride: from walking-on-air, ready-to-take-on-the-world excitement, to a moment or two of nervous quiet when the voice in your head said "Holy crap, NOW what?!?"

Well, rest a bit easier – this book is EXACTLY for you.

What You'll Want to Know

There are a million things we COULD cover, which is why there's about a million management books out there. I'm going to stick to the truly important stuff, the stuff I wish I'd known when I first became a manager.

First, we'll cover what's different about your world now than before. What does the management role entail, how is it different from what you used to do on a daily basis, and some of the sticking points or pitfalls you will likely run into.

Then, we'll get into The Most Basic Thing You Need to Know (how's THAT for a tease, eh?) If you can get this right, REALLY right, you will immediately be far, far ahead of the curve, and in truth, better than the great majority of managers out there. Seriously.

We'll also walk you through a little self-introspection; have you think about what YOU might want out of this whole adventure and examine some of your goals and aspirations.

Then, it's nitty-gritty time; we'll take a look at my 10 for 90 – the ten items on your to-do list for the first ninety days in your new role. Nothing, and I mean nothing, is more critical than acting like a leader from Day One:

> **"Men make history and not the other way around. In periods where there is no leadership, society stands still. Progress occurs when courageous, skillful leaders seize the opportunity to change things for the better."**
> **— Harry S. Truman**

The 10 for 90 will help you look, and more importantly, feel the confidence a leader needs because it'll give you a practical, <u>actionable</u> path to follow that will get you jump-started toward real success.

After that, we'll look beyond the first ninety days and at the larger context of leadership, how you can fit into it, and how you can join what can be a new kind of leadership that will lead us all to a more humane and inspiring way to work. You can help change the world while you "duke it out" in the reality of the everyday.

A little grandiose, you say? You just want some basic info you can use, everyday stuff? No big deal. Okay, fair enough; you *will* find that here. But "everyday stuff" ain't the whole picture; it ain't "no big deal". Maybe I am a bit over the top on this one, but I don't see it that way. If you can't find a bigger cause to serve, a reason to get out of bed in the morning, why bother? The world DOES desperately need a new kind of manager that can grow businesses AND inspire people – and when you can be the leader that does it ends up a big(!) win for everyone. Businesses are better; lives are better.

Grandiose? Maybe. But only a smidge.

Besides, as they say, go big or go home!

….Okay, so much for the chit-chat. Let's get to it.

Manager? Or Leader?

The popular phrase that's been going around for a long, long time is "Managers do things right; leaders do the right things". This is interesting, and rolls off the tongue nicely, but it's not accurate. The implication here is that managers tend merely to the day-to-day details and leaders somehow have mystical views of the future. As I said, wrong, wrong, wrong.

Managers DO tend to focus on the day-to-day, the nitty-gritty stuff that gets task A done, then task B done, etc. That's what the job is. But what is a leader? We tend to use the phrase "leader" to imply someone with a high-level executive job, like a CEO, who sits in his or her office all day thinking deep thoughts about what the organization needs to do, how it needs to act, and how it needs to grow and change to a well-defined future state.

But that's often wrong, too. Many CEOs today are overly focused on the short-term, not the long-term (more on this in a bit).

So a leader is not determined by his or her title or position, but by their attitude, perspective, and outlook. You can be a leader as an administrative assistant, you can be a leader as a member of your IT systems administration group, and you can surely be a leader as a new manager.

And that's what we so desperately need today, leaders not merely managers.

Managers...

- Worry about getting the XYZ report out on time.
- Keep track of when their people come in each day, when they go to lunch, when they go home.
- Follow the process (to deal with an issue, to grant vacation time, to get results out of their employees) to the letter, so that they are always "covered"
- Tend to treat their staff as a means to an end, as tools to get the work done.
- Tend to focus on themselves and how what's happening (good or bad) reflects on them and their career prospects.

Leaders (true leaders, that is)...

- Value the people they work with, and place them first on the priority list; THEN customers/clients.

- They pay attention not only to the "hard stuff" (productivity metrics, quality, cost) but also to the "soft stuff" – people management, people optimization, and people growth.
- Look at processes and always ask "why" – why are we doing this? Why are we doing this in this way? Does this process make the best use of our people? Could it be done better? (And, oh by the way, they will include their people, the ones actually doing the work, in this question and answer process. After all, a great many processes look great from the manager's chair but can make little or no sense from the people who actually have to live with it every day).
- Have maximizing their people's potential as a "top-of-mind" item.
- Think bigger picture: how this group/function fits within the bigger picture of the organization, and how this might change going forward based on the changes in the industry and the world at large.

I've painted the manager vs. leader thing in pretty broad strokes here to make the point. All managers are not calculating, Scrooge-like selfish CYA'ers, and all leaders are not virtuous warm-and-fuzzy people lovers. Leaders, just like the managers, make sure the XYZ report gets out on time and that it doesn't have errors. They make sure their staff follows organizational procedures. It's a matter of HOW they go about it that makes all the difference. To sum it up, a manager will more than likely tell his staffer Jim, "Here's how we need the XYZ report to get done. We do this, and that, and the other thing. It needs to be out by 9 a.m. each morning without errors. Two errors in a month and I'll have to write you up. I'll be watching. And oh by the way, the quality metrics will be part of your annual performance appraisal." A leader will approach it more like this: "Jim, our XYZ report goes to the purchasing department and since they use it to make buying decisions we need to get them the most accurate numbers we can. Jane will walk you through how we do the report today but we're always looking to make it easier and better, so any ideas you may have will be appreciated. If you have any questions make sure you talk with Jane."

The point of the examples is not to bash managers. I can hear some of you managers saying, "Hey, wait a minute – you're making us look like cold-hearted unfeeling jerks. We're not like that." No, of course there are some great managers. My point though is one of mindset and perspective: managers tend to be tactical, by-the-rules people. Leaders tend to be more people-focused and more broad-based (strategic) in their thinking, with a strong predilection not only for getting the work done, but getting it done in the most productive way possible by means of tapping in to all the skills and talents of their people.

Look at it this way: Encouraging people and creating a culture of contribution to make things better fully engages their head, heart, and soul in what they do every day. In return, someone who leads in this way engenders tremendous loyalty in their team, and they will be motivated to give their very best effort to the leader and the team, far beyond what it would take to just keep their job. This is referred to as "discretionary effort" and we will explore it in depth in Chapter 3.

What do YOU want to become? A manager or a true leader?

Your answer is more important than you might think.

Why We Absolutely Need You Now

People-centric leadership is nothing new; but it is much rarer than it used to be, and getting rarer. We've already mentioned the toll that pursuing "shareholder value" has taken on valuing people, there is also the ongoing pressure of globalization which, along with misguided U.S. trade policy and short-term thinking, is causing an overall environment of fear in the workplace. That fear is contributing to what is being called a "crisis of competence" both in the private and public sectors.

> Back in December [2008], veteran foreign correspondent William Pfaff asked the right question: How much faith do other states still have in American competence?

> Back in 2005, the failed occupation in Iraq and the bungled response to Hurricane Katrina led many foreign observers to question whether America's leaders knew what they were doing. The aura of effectiveness matters, because American influence depends in good part on the belief that U.S. leaders (both public and private) are knowledgeable, honest, and above all competent individuals who can figure out what needs to be done and then actually get it implemented.

> Today, however, the drip-drip-drip of bad news and the growing sense that malfeasance and moral rot are widespread risks permanent damage to America's global image …add to that the Wall Street meltdown, the Madoff scandal, the Blagojevich follies, and the Big 3 automakers' lame

pleas, and you have a picture of America that raises more doubts than hopes.[1]

So this is the mess we've gotten into. This is the world of business today and the state of leadership. Previous leadership "generations" have, as a group, lost their way and ours. As a whole, American organizations are less competitive, less strong, and have created a culture of fear in their employees that has led them to leave their heads, hearts, and souls at home.

Their time is waning. We need a new set of leaders that can engage and inspire a workforce just waiting to belong to organizations they believe in, something larger than themselves, and someplace they can contribute in a meaningful long-term way.

> To cut costs, companies have been repeatedly downsized, and the mindsets and attitudes of employees – both those that were victimized and those who survived – have been permanently scarred. Company loyalty as it used to be is a thing of the past. Employees have been forced to learn that their first loyalty must be to themselves.....Work without soul is spirit-destroying. Business without committed people is doomed to mediocrity and ultimately failure. This is the legacy shareholder value thinking and the short-termism has left for future generations. [2]

That's why I've written this book: I believe we need a new generation of leaders that know how to inspire their teams/groups/ organizations to great things, to see and help realize the nearly unlimited potential of their people, and revitalize organizations in a way that is humane and meaningful.

Dee Hock, the founder of Visa, summed it up in his book *One From Many: VISA and the rise of chaordic organization:*

To be precise, one cannot speak of leaders who cause organizations to achieve superlative performance, for no one can cause it to happen. Leaders can only recognize and modify conditions that prevent it; perceive and articulate a sense of community, a vision of the future, a body of principle to which people can become passionately committed, then encourage and enable them to discover and bring forth the extraordinary capabilities that lie trapped in everyone struggling to get out.

People are not things to be manipulated, labeled, boxed, bought, and sold. Above all else, they are not human resources. They are entire human beings, containing the whole of the evolving universe, limitless until we start limiting them. We must examine the concept of leading and following with new eyes. We must examine the concept of superior and subordinate with increasing skepticism. We must examine the concept of management and labor with new beliefs. And we must examine the nature of organizations that demand such distinctions with an entirely different consciousness.

It is true leadership; leadership by everyone; leadership in, up, around, and down this world so badly needs, and dominator management it so sadly gets.``

You, the new manager/leader, can make a difference by making the choice to become part of the new generation that takes us all to a better, more productive, more humane future.

Are you in? Then turn the page.

Recap & Things to Remember (T.T.R.)

- This book will give you new perspectives and actionable suggestions on all the key things a new manager like you needs to be successful.

- The 10 for 90 will give you an effective roadmap to propel you to success in the next ninety days.

- Aspire to be a leader, not a manager; managers focus on the tactical, leaders go beyond the tactical, looking to always improve what happens today and what will be needed tomorrow.

- "People stuff" may be a "soft" topic, but there's literally power in the people "Discretionary Effort" is real, and in today's world is being left at home. Be the kind of leader that taps into that power.

- Previous leadership "generations" have helped to create a crisis of competence and an overall culture of fear. It's up to you, one of the New Leadership generation, to begin the movement for change...

Chapter Notes

[1]Stephen M. Walt, "The Crisis of Competence", Foreign Policy, January 15, 2009 (http://walt.foreignpolicy.com/posts/2009/01/15/the_crisis_of_competence)

[2]Terrence E. Dela and Alan A. Kennedy, *The New Corporate Cultures*, Perseus Publishing, 1999. Chapter 2.

CHAPTER 2

YIKES!

*Get involved in something that you care so much about that you
want to make it the greatest it can possibly be, not because of
what you will get, but just because it can be done.*

*—Jim Collins, Good to Great: Why Some Companies Make the
Leap... and Others Don't*

What Got You Here Ain't Gonna Keep You Here

You're a newly-minted manager/leader. You more than likely were placed into this position because of several or all of the following reasons:

- Your boss likes you
- You have a good attitude
- You're a great team player
- You have good ideas
- You show potential for leadership
- You have a track record of achievement
- You're attained a level of expertise and excellence in your old role

It's also likely that the last three items were the most important considerations in you getting the promotion into your new role.

However, there's a problem with this, a major glitch.

And that is: the job you've been so good at isn't your job anymore.

What You Used to Do, What You're Doing Now

Your job used to be as a "doer", an executor, or an "individual contributor", as per the current buzzword phrase. You collaborated. You had a series of tasks to do, and working together (hopefully!) with others you got the work and the job done.

Now you're stepping into a different world; not just a different role but a different KIND of role.

In your old role, you were primarily responsible for yourself, and the work you did. You were given assignments and handled them. Now, if you're a "pure" manager, you're no longer the one doing the work at all, you are responsible for a team that does the work. If your new role is more the "team lead" type of role, you'll have some tasks that you'll still do but you have additional staff that you're responsible for. Whatever comes out of your team, however much they produce and how well they produce it, is up to you; the buck stops at your desk. You're now responsible for answering questions, assigning tasks, assessing progress, providing guidance, and reviewing your team's individual achievements in their personnel reviews, and more. In sum, the bulk of your daily work is no longer performing tasks, it's directing and monitoring the efforts of others.

It's a whole new game, and it's a people game.

The Pull of the Familiar

Because it's a whole new game, there's a lot for you to learn. In some cases, it's the complete opposite side of the brain that's doing the work. To illustrate, the table below summarizes the various tasks controlled by each side of our brains:[1]

LEFT BRAIN FUNCTIONS	RIGHT BRAIN FUNCTIONS
uses logic	uses feeling
detail oriented	"big picture" oriented
facts rule	imagination rules
words and language	symbols and images
math and science	philosophy and religion
can comprehend	can "get it" (i.e. meaning)
knowing	believes
knows object name	knows object function
forms strategies	presents possibilities

The takeaway here is that in your old role you were heavily "left brain" oriented, but your new role is much more "right brain" oriented, and by definition then your thought processes are completely different. Also by definition, it probably won't feel comfortable at all and it may feel very foreign to you. This is very normal, but it is the first major challenge you'll face as a manager/leader – can you make the leap to this new way of thinking and acting?

Because of this, you will be tempted, and drawn back to your old ways and your old ways of thinking. You may find yourself feeling swamped as you try to handle all the work of your team. If you're now leading a team that's in the same area you used to work in, you may even find yourself actually <u>doing your old job</u>.

Don't let this all-too-common mistake happen to you. In your first few weeks or months of being a leader, if what you're doing at any particular moment feels as comfortable as your favorite shoes, stop yourself and think about what you're doing. If it's <u>that</u> comfortable, it's probably because you're doing something more like your old job than your new one. So do your new job. Delegate the work you're doing to someone on your team. If no one knows how, teach them. It's the only way to move on, to become the leader we need you to be and you want to become.

Bottom line: if it's familiar, if it's comfortable, then it's probably not something you should be doing.

Other Common Mistakes

Before I outline what I think your new job REALLY is, I wanted to insert a short cautionary note here. Although the Familiarity Trap is one of the most significant pitfalls you'll face, there are a number of other possible mistakes that can trip you up. Without making this chapter a complete downer, I'll limit this to the top ten.

Top 10 New Manager Mistakes [2]

1. Think you know everything.
2. Show everyone who's in charge.
   a. While it IS necessary to carry yourself like a leader from day one, be careful not to overdo it. Everybody, and I mean everybody, will notice that you're trying too hard, and it will make everyone think you're insecure. Take a softer approach, at least until you know more about your team and your area.
3. Change everything.
   a. Take the time to figure out what's working and what isn't. Make a list and prioritize it in order of importance and tackle them in order. One change well implemented is MUCH better than ten changes all done badly. Give yourself early wins.

4. Be afraid to do anything.
5. Don't take time to get to know your people.
    a. We've touched on this already, and will cover the "people thing" in more detail in Chapter 3.
6. Ignore your boss.
7. Don't worry about problems or problem employees.
    a. See you in Chapter 3!
8. Don't let yourself be human.
9. Don't protect your people.
10. Avoid responsibility for anything.
    a. This is at the very core of your new role. Responsibility is what your new job is ALL about; better you learn that now. Suck it up and deal; the buck stops at your desk now!

What Your New Job REALLY Is

If you're going to be a leader, you need to be all about the people who report to you. (Did you notice that four of the Top 10 New Manager Mistakes had to do with people issues? Go back and check it out!) From your boss's standpoint, you've been entrusted with a task large enough that needs other people to get it done, and he/she thinks you're up to the task. From a more abstract standpoint, though, you've been given access to a great multiplier effect – you, working with other people, can get many times more work done than you yourself can do alone. Your work is now judged by how well you can work with your people to make things happen. The better they are, the better you, and your team, are.

Tom Peters, a long-time management expert and author of a number of great books on the subject (start with his seminal effort, *In Search of Excellence*, and you'll be a better leader for it), has made presentation slides available on his website that he uses in his seminars. On the topic of managing people he says[3]:

> # Hard" stuff/analysis and planning:
>
> ## 25%
>
> ## Soft" stuff/people and Politics and passion and execution:
>
> ## 75%

Think about this hard, and take it to heart. Being a good leader isn't about being the "biggest dog" in the room. Being a good leader doesn't come with great genius, great connections, an accident of birth or because your dad owns the company. Being a good leader is not about charisma.

It's much simpler than that: treat your people as human beings, as family. Does that sound weird, lame, or weak? It may sound that way to you. But nothing could be further from the truth. Leaders, TRUE leaders, embrace (and live) the idea of servant leadership.

"Sure", you say, "but isn't that all warm-and-fuzzy HR stuff? I work in manufacturing (or construction, or any other hard-edged, macho industry you might name, up to and including the military). That stuff won't fly where I work."

Wrong.

The Marines have a saying: "Officers eat last." The Corps knows ALL ABOUT servant leadership, and the power it can create. How many times have you heard of the Marine Corps mentioned in the context of organizations with a great history and great morale? There's a reason for the morale.

And how about Jack Welch, former CEO of General Electric and Herb Kelleher, former CEO of Southwest Airlines? It could be argued that these two CEOs belong in the team photo of the most effective leaders of the past twenty-five years, both in industries not kind to lightweights or fuzzy thinkers. And they both say nearly the same thing.

First, Welch:
"On the face of it, shareholder value is the dumbest idea in the world. Shareholder value is a result, not a strategy. ...Your main constituencies are your employees, your customers and your products."[4]
Then Kelleher:

"If the employees come first, then they're happy, ... A motivated employee treats the customer well. The customer is happy so they keep coming back, which pleases the shareholders. It's not one of the enduring Green mysteries of all time; it is just the way it works."[5]

That, then, is what your new role REALLY is all about: maximizing the potential and performance of your people not as a domineering ringmaster, but as a coach. One key thing to remember is that coaches don't motivate, they <u>inspire</u>.

Recap & T.T.R.

- What you used to do is likely nothing like what you're supposed to be doing now.
- It probably requires you to use the opposite side of your brain and it ain't comfortable; it shouldn't be.
- Beware the Familiarity Trap; if it feels comfortable, you probably shouldn't be doing it.
- Your new role has (very) little to do with tasks; it's about the people.

Chapter Notes

[1]Dan Eden, "Left Brain, Right Brain", (http://viewzone2.com/bicamx.html)

[2]F. John Reh, "The Top 10 New Manager Mistakes", http://management.about.com/od/begintomanage/tp/newmgrmistake.htm

[3]Tom Peters, Event Slides, www.tompeters.com

[4]Financial Times, March 13, 2009, p. 1

[5]Tom Peters, Event Slides, www.tompeters.com

CHAPTER 3

SERVE THOSE THAT SERVE YOU

If you want your employees to be completely devoted to you and your cause, you must first be completely devoted to them.

— *Simon Sinek, Starting With Why*

If You Never Learn Anything Else About Leading, Learn This

We began to touch on this in Chapter 2, however I will expand on it here. The ONE thing to learn about being a leader is simple and straightforward, but I can't tell you how many leaders never, ever, EVER get it. Here it is:

People come first.

Or alternatively,

It ain't about you anymore;
It's about them.

Everything you do and everything you will achieve as a leader, happens through your people and the people they work with in other teams and departments. Treat them well and they will reward you, treat them like crap and they will at best do only as much as they need to, or at worst actively work to sabotage you.

As a new leader, you now either have the real title with the explicit authority or no real title but with new implicit authority. Either way, you now have some real control over the people who now report to you.

In the remainder of this chapter, we'll explore several concepts of leadership that may not be evident to you, things that are not a part of what you've ever envisioned about "leadership". That's okay; don't be concerned. Truth be told, many, many managers/

leaders out there don't get ANY of what you're about to learn. But this stuff is EXACTLY what is needed today from people who want to be truly effective, enduring, influential, and most of all inspiring leaders.

We'll kick things off discussing the concept of "Level 5 leadership", which came out of author Jim Collins' 2001 book *Good to Great*, which, as he discovered through meticulous research, is one of the key determining factors whether or not an organization moves past mediocrity. Then we'll look at the idea of servant leadership, or as this chapter's heading indicates, serving those that serve you. We'll also cover the very important concept of discretionary effort, what it means to you, and what you can do to maximize it.

Key Concept: Level 5 Leadership

Collins' book *Good to Great* is a useful reference book because it is not conjecture or opinion. It is first and foremost a research work, encapsulating years of study on public companies to find out what makes a company go from good, or even mediocre, to great? Collins compared these companies to others in the SAME industries/timeframe/markets and were roughly the same size at the outset of the study yet did not make the same leap to greatness. Why? Their first comparison criterion, not surprisingly, addressed the leadership of those companies vs. those they were compared against. What the research found was that the companies that became great had within them a pyramid of leadership capabilities Collins summed this up as follows:

Level 1: Highly Capable Individual

Level 2: Contributing Team Member

Level 3: Competent Manager

Level 4: Effective Leader

Level 5: Level 5 Executive[1]

Before I make my point here, let me give you the definitions Collins gives to the top three levels.

I. Competent Manager: Organizes people and resources toward the effective and efficient pursuit of predetermined objectives.

II. Effective Leader: Catalyzes commitment to and vigorous pursuit of a clear and compelling vision, stimulating higher performance standards.

III. Level 5 Leader: Builds enduring greatness through a paradoxical blend of personal humility and professional will.[2]

An aside here.... Of these three leadership types, which one would you really want to be like? Which one would you want leading YOU? Which level would inspire you? Which one would get you out of bed at 6 a.m. in the middle of January?

What Collins and his research team found is that, bar none, all of the "great" organizations had a Level 5 leader, one who had a very strong sense of humility, that is, very little ego. She/he was not looking to toot their own horn, or to be the showy, charismatic CEO we all seem to think of when we imagine great leaders. The Level 5 leaders also, without exception, had an incredible will, a steely-eyed focus on absolutely, positively making their organization grow, become better, and meet its potential for greatness.

From Collins himself:

> "The essential difference between the '5' and the '4' was surprising. The '5' was the *antithesis* of the great egocentric leader. The '5' was the leader who operated, first and foremost, with a genuine humility. But it was humility defined as a burning, passionate, obsessive ambition for the cause, for the company, for the work – not themselves. And they had this utterly stoic will to make good on that ambition."[3]

Great leaders are that way because they're not out to make themselves great, they're out to make the organization/cause great. This is precisely why people follow them. This is precisely why they inspire over long periods of time. Which is why people are motivated to give their best day after day. Nothing kills inspiration and effort faster than a leader who appears to be looking out for number one. People sniff that out in about thirty seconds and stop responding.

So you have a choice to make. Who are you out for? Is your passion for you/yourself or for the mission, vision, or the betterment of your group? It's the oddest of paradoxes: if you want to be an exceptional leader, you need to care more for your group's success than you do your own.

We'll touch on this again later. But for now you'd do well to keep this in mind: in the 2005 movie *Miracle*, USA Olympic hockey coach Herb Brooks (played by Kurt Russell) tells his 1980s squad, "The name on the <u>front</u> of the jersey [USA] is a hell of a lot more important than the name on the <u>back</u>!"

Key Concept: Servant Leadership

The "humility" aspect of Level 5 leadership is a direct offshoot of the idea of leader as servant.

This is hardly a new concept. A quick survey of the New Testament is peppered with language and vignettes describing how Jesus led as servant leadership. Martin Luther King and Mother Teresa are two modern examples.

But the concept need not be exclusive to religious circles. In fact, the term "servant leadership" was coined in 1970 by a businessman – retired AT&T executive Robert K. Greenleaf. He outlined the concept in an essay he wrote titled *The Servant Leader.*

"The servant-leader *is* servant first... It begins with the natural feeling that one wants to serve, to serve *first*. Then conscious choice brings one to aspire to lead. That person is sharply different from one who is *leader* first, perhaps because of the need to assuage an unusual power drive or to acquire material possessions...The leader-first and the servant-first are two extreme types. Between them there are shadings and blends that are part of the infinite variety of human nature.

"The difference manifests itself in the care taken by the servant-first to make sure that other people's highest priority needs are being served. The best test, and difficult to administer, is: Do those served grow as persons? Do they, *while being served*, become healthier, wiser, freer, more autonomous, more likely themselves to become servants?"[4]

Greenleaf wrote this over forty years ago, in part to address what he saw as a lack of this kind of leadership. *Forty years.*

So if it's such an old concept, one that's identified with some of the most influential leaders in history, why do we (still!) see so little of it?

Good question; I don't have a definitive answer. I do, however, have some observations. One of the first traits working against servant leadership is the ego of the new leader. They likely spent a significant amount of time, years maybe, working their way up the ladder. They may feel that the "lower-level" jobs they held along the way were somehow demeaning, and used the vision of "making it" to drive them to ultimately achieve a leadership role. Now finally in a leadership job they feel they've ascended to a new level, "out of the soup" so to speak, and are now somehow better than the people reporting to them and that these folks have roles meant to serve as tools for continued advancement. Because of this feeling, leaders like this focus primarily on results, usually monetary, so that they can wrangle that NEXT promotion, that next raise, and that next larger office. In this scenario people are no longer teammates; they're merely a means to an end.

Unfortunately for most of us, this behavior is condoned, encouraged, and perpetuated by their bosses, who regard this kind of management as a good thing. It's likely how THEY got to where they are, too.

The second reason servant leadership isn't more prevalent is that many people seek leadership for power; power over budgets, power over situations, power over people. They want to be leaders PURELY for what it gets them and this is therefore the very antithesis of leadership. It's also a very binary relationship – if I'm the leader and you're not, I have power and you don't. These kinds of leaders tend to be very directorial, even dictatorial, giving their staffs very little room for individual contribution; it's "my way or the highway".

Another main reason servant leadership is not more common is that it is seen as "soft" (that is, not grounded in logic or numbers) and somehow wimpy. It may seem that way, given our fascination with charismatic, strong-and-silent-type leaders. The perception of those leaders is, "How can I be IN CHARGE, how will they know I'm the leader if I'm serving my people? We need to run a tight ship around here to make the numbers." This is really nothing but a case of where perception does not fit with reality. Yes, these kinds of leaders can get results; results that quickly turn around a floundering organization and get all kinds of attention in the media as the new "Wonder Girl" that saved the company. Yes, this kind of thing happens, and can inspire us. But the reality is that this kind of leadership <u>doesn't last</u>. The (hard) numbers are there. The "comparison" companies in Good to Great had short term success, but without Level 5/servant leadership that success either didn't last or <u>never happened</u>. Southwest Airlines is another example. I've quoted Herb Kelleher earlier; he was clearly focused on serving his employees first – and Southwest has turned a profit thirty-five years(!) in a row, in an industry rife with bankruptcies and forced mergers.

The final (and perhaps biggest) reason for the dearth of servant leadership is trust. That is, the leader trusting her people. I've seen many, many times where people have been promoted to leadership positions primarily on the strength of their ability to keep track of, and control, large amounts of information and tasks. They are the very definition of "detail-oriented". This can be a tremendous asset as an individual contributor, but can be a huge problem for a leader, especially if the leader cannot bring herself to trust her people. This is where micro-managers come from, and if you've ever worked for one you know how awful it can be.

The leader in effect tells her people to check their brains at the door each morning so they are able to do whatever the leader has told them to. If the leader's area is small, or the leader is truly brilliant, this mode can actually work for a while, but ultimately the employees will leave. The high turnover makes the leader's job more difficult, and only tends to perpetuate the leader's notion that "everyone is unreliable". These leaders can actually hang on for some time in larger, more bureaucratic organizations, but they will always limit their ability to create a truly productive team and will end up doing much more harm than good.

Trust is the key to avoid all this. I'm not advocating BLIND trust, that's just silly. You as a leader must trust in your people to do the right thing, but they may need help, monitoring, and coaching to get there. THAT's how you serve. Give them the information, the tools, and the latitude to do what they need to do, and then get the hell out of their way.

The key components of servant leadership are:

- Listening (actively)
- Empathy
- Healing
- Awareness
- Persuasion
- Conceptualization
- Foresight
- Stewardship
- Commitment to the growth of people
- Building a community[5]

The full description of all of these qualities is beyond the scope of this book, but there are a number of places for you to get more information to expand your knowledge of this critical concept. See the Chapter Notes.

In short, though, the whole concept of servant leadership is to remove barriers. If you've got the people behind you and have built up trust with them, your job is to help them help you. Make that phone call to your colleague in the Shipping Department to clear the way for someone on your team to get something out the door on time. Kick down the hurdles that your staff may not be able to. They'll love you for it; they'll get results, which are in effect results for you. Your team will get a reputation for getting things done and people will want to work for you. Everybody wins. Big.

Key Concept: Discretionary Effort

Discretionary effort is a hundred-dollar MBA term for something we've all seen almost every working day. It is as familiar as it is insidious.

Discretionary effort is the phenomenon in which "People regulate the amount of effort they put into their jobs based on how well they feel they're being treated by their boss."[6]

Furthermore, "If they feel they're being treated well, they will become excited about giving their absolute best efforts, which means they'll work way beyond their job descriptions. If they feel their efforts are unappreciated, they'll pull back and do only what they have to do to keep their jobs. And if they feel they're being abused, they'll either get even by figuring out a way to sabotage their boss's performance numbers, or they'll look for a job somewhere else."[7]

This isn't pretty, but it is real. Anybody who tells you this doesn't happen is telling you the biggest fib in the history of the human race. We've all seen it; some of us have actually done this. There has been a few times, earlier in my own career, that I've actually *done* this. Not that I ever sabotaged my boss, but I did scale back my efforts and put them into finding a new job. I'm not real proud of it, but as a new manager you have to realize that this happens. You can avoid it easily enough by treating your people well. The closer you can get to Level 5/servant leadership, the better chance that this will never be an issue for you.

In summary, then, as a leader you need to create an environment where your team is valued and allowed to bring themselves and their brains to work. In turn you will receive their discretionary effort, which in effect is a gift from them to you.

> "...Loyalty is the conscious decision of stakeholders – employee, customer, supplier, investor – to actively invest themselves in a voluntary relationship. Loyal stakeholders give gifts of themselves to companies they feel have earned them. For example, stellar employee performance is not an obligation, but a choice on the part of the employee. In most situations, an employee can easily keep her job by doing no more than her employer requires. Thus, if she keeps the company's best interests in mind instead, it is a gift."[8]

The essence of leadership is very basic. You need to have people who want to follow you. Willingly. The key question is: would they follow you if you didn't have a title?

Key Concept: Tapping Into & Maximizing Your Team's Potential

By now you're likely becoming convinced of the productivity, the downright power, and inspiration of leading others in a way that values them.

With that, a key perspective that helps drive the whole picture is the leader looking at their team not just as executors of tasks, but as almost *unlimited reservoirs of potential*. Logically, of course, for any particular task or situation, some of us have more potential at that task and at that moment than others, but for a different task at a different time their potential may be much higher. Logic aside, though, it is very empowering to your people if you view them as if they have what it takes or can grow into what you need them to do. In some cases they may fall short, but in my perspective most of them will indeed rise to the occasion and surprise not only you but themselves. And oddly enough, no matter how hard it may have been for them, they will invariably thank YOU for the chance. They will feel as if you saw something in them that perhaps they did not, and the feeling of pride and accomplishment they feel will fuel them on to even bigger and better achievements. Nothing creates that strong feeling of team, loyalty, pride, and sense of belonging to a great group than seeing the potential in your people. It pulls together all the elements we've been exploring, from Level 5 to servant leadership to trusting your people. It all comes down to believing in your folks and then letting them do their damndest to prove you right.

People want to be part of something larger than themselves. They want to be part of something they're really proud of, that they'll fight for, sacrifice for, that they trust.

— Howard Schultz, Starbucks

Recap & T.T.R.

- Put your people first. **Period**.
- Humility + Will = Level 5 Leadership.
- Go out and get yourself a copy of Collins' *Good to Great*. It's one of the best business books ever and reading it is the equivalent of an MBA course.
- More words from Dee Hock, former Chairman of VISA: "Ph.D. in leadership, Short Course: Make a short list of all things done to you that you abhorred. Don't do them to others. Ever. Make another list of things done to you that you loved. Do them to others. Always." *Memorize* this; make it a part of your everyday practice. If you do, you'll become a better leader than ninety percent of those out there.
- Continuously view your people as nearly bottomless reservoirs of potential. Help them, coach them, trust them, and let them work like hell to prove you right.

Chapter Notes

[1]Jim Collins, Good to Great, HarperCollins, 2001, p. 20.
[2]Ibid.
[3]From a video clip on Jim Collins' website: http://www.jimcollins.com/media_topics/level-5.html#audio=81
[4]The Greenleaf Center for Servant Leadership website, http://www.greenleaf.org/whatissl/. This site is a great place to get started with

the concept; they have links to a number of books and white papers on the topic.

[5]Servant Leadership video, http://www.youtube.com/watch?v=OH d7s2OzpVI&feature=results_main&playnext=1&list=PLD1CB9806 7C8E02F5

[6]Harry Paul and Ron Reck, Ph.D., *Instant Turnaround! Getting People Excited About Coming to Work and Working Hard*, William Morrow, 2009, Chapter 4.

[7]Ibid.

[8]Tom Decotiis, Make It Glow: How to Build a Company Reputation for Human Goodness, Flawless Execution, and Being Best –in-Class, Greenleaf Book Group, 2008, Chapter 1.

Chapter 4

THE MIRROR CHECK

OR

PARDON ME, YOUR "WHO" IS SHOWING

Take a *Good* Look....

So you're a new manager who thinks they want to be a leader.

You're stepping into a world you've never lived in but only seen from the outside where you've watched other people manage/lead. By definition, you don't have a real clue.

Over the course of the rest of this book we'll get to the "what" of being an exceptional leader. But first, you need to take a minute to take stock of who YOU are, and assess how well you stack up against the demands this new role will make of you.

In effect, you'll be interviewing yourself. I've made it easy for you; I'm giving you the questions.

In the next section I list what I consider the most important bare-bulb-in-the-interrogation-room questions you're going to need to know the answers for. Imagine yourself a ten-year veteran at this leadership thing, interviewing a candidate for a key leadership role in your organization. These are the questions you'd want to ask that candidate, but let's start by seeing how YOU do answering them first.

Is this an exhaustive list? No. Just the most important.

In an unscientific, I-know-it-when-I-see-it way, the more solid "yes" answers you can give to the Top 20 the better leader you will likely be. As you answer, be careful of just breezing through them chalking up "yes" after "yes" just to give yourself a great score. For some of the questions I'll give you some real-life situations to make you think a little longer about them.

Take for instance question five, "Can you trust?" Your first reaction might be to jump to the yes answer, citing all the times in your life you were an incredibly trusting individual. But what if the situation was such that you had a difficult assignment ahead, one that you would have to delegate to someone on your team. Let's say that on paper the right person for the job was Jackie, one of your team that had the drive and the potential, but had demonstrated an uncanny ability in the past to screw things up. Let's also say the assignment is VERY visible to senior management, so a good result helps your standing, your image, and you career, but a bad result would mean major-league egg on your face, possibly no raise, or even a reprimand from your boss. Okay, hotshot, NOW can you trust Jackie with the assignment?

In this example, the answer is "it depends". At this point in the real-life scenario a better question might be "What would it take for you to trust?" That question might lead you to an answer, "Well, if I knew she wouldn't screw up the relationship with Accounting, I'd feel pretty good about giving her this assignment." And maybe you have someone on your team, good ol' Fred, who spent five years in Accounting and is still close with most of them. Maybe you assign ol' Fred to Jackie to help her work with Accounting to make sure things stay on course there. Have you trusted? Yes. Have you taken a chance in trusting Jackie that a less secure, less trusting manager would assign? Yup. Have you blindly trusted just to be a great guy or gal? Hardly. You're giving Jackie the assignment, which will allow Jackie to grow, but you mitigate her biggest weakness. You've altered the situation to remove much of the risk and set EVERYONE up for success. Does Jackie still need to learn how to deal with Accounting? Sure. But you can do that on some other project, one without the high stakes and visibility this one has.

One question down, nineteen more to go in your self-interview. Not exactly the cakewalk you might've expected, eh?

These questions, and their answers, are the difference between being an exceptional leader and a bad one. Why should you care? Because exceptional leaders change lives, empower people, change the world. Bad leaders increase stress, ruin self-esteem, ruin marriages, ruin lives, ruin companies. You pick.

The Top 20 Questions: Being a Leader

1. Are you all about people?
   By definition, your new job is to get things done using the people now entrusted to you. The better a people-person you can be will let you understand these people, find what inspires and motivates them, and then let them do it. More on this later.

2. Can you check your ego at the door?
   Hint: If you answer "no" to this, you've got yourself a problem. Sure, everyone has an ego, and to get where you are right now you had to have a well-developed one. But if you continue to feed it, keeping yourself first on your list, you will fail. Your focus now needs to be on your team, your staff and their performance, now and into the future.

3. Can you be unpopular?
   Many times, doing what's right may not be the most popular thing in the world. Are you in this to have people over you all the time, or do you want to achieve something? This may be a more difficult answer if the person you're ticking off is the close colleague you've worked with for years. How strong is your backbone?

4. Can you be decisive with limited information?
   In my experience getting the first eighty percent of the information you need to make a decision is relatively quick and relatively easy. The last twenty percent or so may take days or weeks (if it's even possible). How comfortable are you with making a decision with only eighty percent of the information. (Note: waiting the extra time for that last twenty percent is ALMOST ALWAYS a bad idea.)

5. Can you trust?
   See my earlier scenario with Jackie and Fred.

6. Can you be truly responsible?
   If you want to be an exceptional leader, you need to be truly responsible. Many decisions now will come to rest on your desk looking for an answer. If you assign James to a task and he flubs it, within your team you must address it as an issue for James, but if his screw-up has external ramifications, YOU must take the blame. Publicly hanging James out to dry may be factually accurate, but nothing will lose a team member's loyalty faster than the feeling they won't be supported by the boss.

7. Can you embrace failure?
    Trying to be perfect, and have your team be perfect, is a fool's pursuit. You'll have to keep in mind your corporate culture here, but the more you can embrace (intelligent) failure the faster you will get to the right answer every time. We humans learn best by trying, messing up, trying again, messing up again, and then getting it right.

8. Can you be a coach?
    The leader-as-coach metaphor is a very good one. You're not a boss, you're not a director, and you're not there to do their jobs for them. To use a sports example, you never saw coach Phil Jackson of the L.A. Lakers tell Kobe Bryant how to shoot; but he WOULD tell Kobe how to read defenses better, how to avoid the double-team, or give him a tip on how to beat a pick. Kobe could be Kobe, bringing his talents to the court; but even with superstars there is room for improvement.

9. Can you be a teacher?
    If you're doing your best to grow your people, there will be many times where you will put your folks in situations where they need help, guidance, and training. You'll need to help them learn and it may be you who has to teach them. This falls right in line with #8 above, because much of what a coach does is teach. You'll need patience, you'll need to see the problem from their perspective as a novice, and you'll need a sincere desire to help them do the task well and do it right. Be (very) careful not to get annoyed at how long this will take – if you don't take the time now, they'll never learn, they'll never grow, and you'll never get out of doing that job. Don't forget to keep checking in with them – or

at least someone else needs to check in with them – to make sure they're succeeding and learning the task correctly. Don't leave them alone to learn it incorrectly!

10. Can you be accountable?

   Let's face it; sometimes even you will screw up. Especially since you're new to this leader thing. Hold yourself to the same, or better yet, higher, standards than that of your team, and if you mess up, show everyone that accountability is for everyone. It's very tempting to give yourself a pass, but don't fall into that trap. Everyone on the team will notice, r find out in less than three seconds via the office grapevine, that somehow the rules don't apply to you. Another loyalty killer.

11. Can you demand excellence?

   If excellence was easy, everyone would be great. Can you set demanding standards and make them stick, even with good ol' everybody's buddy Fred? The hardest part may just be having the will to NOT settle for "good enough".

12. Can you stay out of the details?

   If I had a nickel for every micro-managing boss I've worked for I'd be rich beyond the dreams of avarice. Later we'll get into some more detail on why micro-managers are that way (hint: they can't answer "yes" to a bunch of these questions). You have a staff now to take care of the details. LET THEM. Check on progress toward the details? Sure. Make sure the team knows how to handle the details? No question. Handle them yourself? You'll be tempted, but it's a quick road to leadership disaster.

13. Can you (over)communicate?

    If you think you can just relay information once and have everyone get it right all the time, you're dreaming. And you'll be a lousy leader. Communicate, communicate, communicate some more.

14. Can you inspire?

    Much more on this in Chapter 6, Beyond the 10 for 90. But if you want excellence, if you want a rockin' team, if you want to change the world, you have to inspire people. Why is what they're doing important? Why does your group exist? What larger purpose does it serve? Why should they really, really WANT to get out of bed in the morning to come to work?

15. Do you know when to follow the rules and when not to?

    This is not something you'll be able to learn completely in the first ninety days, but you can get started. Your boss, your organization's culture, and your "relationship" with risk will drive this. The same action taken under two different bosses may have completely different outcomes. Understand what you're getting into. Know the players and the situation as thoroughly as you can. Know what you're going to do and what your rationale will be if you break the rules, get caught, and you're in hot water. Make sure the (potential) reward is worth the risk. Consult a trusted colleague/friend. Then listen to your gut and do what it's telling you.

16. Can you recognize talent and develop it?

    More and more, business is becoming like sports franchises. It's all about the talent, and the best talent wins. Become a student of your team and view them as an almost unlimited reservoir of talent. The more you do this the better you'll get at it. You'll begin to see things in them that they can grow toward that they never saw in themselves. Sometimes all it takes is giving someone a chance that no one else ever did.

17. Can you recognize potential and realize it?
"Potential" and "talent" go hand in hand. And many times both are hidden until a leader can bring it out of someone.

18. Can you think long-term? Define a strategy? Articulate it? Implement it?
Yes, I know, we are very much in a that-was-so-twenty-minutes-ago society and business climate, but that doesn't mean it's a good thing. Focus on today, sure, but make sure you keep a keen watch on what's out there, where you're going, where you SHOULD be going. This allows you to contemplate vision and strategy, which also can help you inspire others.

19. Can you not only keep your head in a crisis, but lead your way out of it?
Listed here as #19, this may be #1 in importance. Do this consistently and you will surely be referred to as a leader, no matter what your title.

20. Can you recognize a poor process? Find a way to improve it? Implement it?
Having the best people on the planet with a crappy process will yield crappy results and miserable people. Think of it as great actors in a movie with a bad script.

Study process, study execution. Know what makes a good process and a bad one, and not just on paper. Too many things sound tremendous on paper and just don't ever work in reality. (For a great and enlightening example of how a bad process can make even great people seem unproductive, Google W. Edwards Deming's red bead experiment.)

This may seem like a daunting list, but don't let it scare you. Doing just a few of these well will make you stand out from most managers/leaders. Once you get over half, people will definitely notice you as a very, very good leader.

Always, always, always keep in mind that you're learning a craft that's not quite like any other. And here's the even-better news...

The 10 Things You GET To Do!

1. Take on ever bigger challenges.
2. Make things better, maybe incredibly better.
3. Improve the working lives of those using your solutions.
4. Save and/or make the company money.
5. Find an issue, set the direction, create the strategy, and get there.
6. Build a team that can take on anything.
7. Help others realize potential in themselves they may not have known they had.
8. Help other people grow, personally and professionally.

9. Inspire people to do something great, something they'll remember fifteen years from now.
10. And yes, sometimes change the world.

My friends, it doesn't get any better than that.

Recap & T.T.R.

- Who you are as a leader is more important than what you know.
- The more of the twenty you are good at, the better a leader you will be. Even being good at a handful of them puts you ahead of most of the managers/leaders out there.
- Use the twenty as a very intense self-interview. Be a tough interviewer and don't cut yourself any slack – after all, you know when you're lying to yourself! The more introspective and detailed you can get, the more you'll learn.
- Study this stuff! There are a zillion leadership books out there; pick a topic you want to improve upon and get after it! Do you want to be an exceptional leader or not?
- Leadership is a craft, an art, and most of all a privilege. Exceptional leaders change the game and move us forward while providing people a chance to be empowered and part of something great and bigger than themselves. Bad leaders ruin...well...everything.

SECTION 2:

GET SET

CHAPTER 5

TO DO LIST: THE 10 FOR 90

We will either find a way, or make one.

— Hannibal

The Critical First 90 Days

The first day you show up to work in your new role, the clock starts ticking. Everyone you regularly come in contact with – your boss, your clients/customers (both inside the company and out) and your colleagues (people and teams you work directly with to get your team's work done) - start watching you. They almost immediately start making judgments about who you are as a new leader, what you're bringing to the table, how you're handling your new responsibility, how you're treating the people you work with, and what you stand for. They're watching and evaluating.

Does that make you nervous? Give you heart palpitations? It's understandable if it does, but not to worry; that's what the 10 for 90 is all about.

For all the reasons above the start to any managerial gig is the most important time. It's the time of first impressions, setting the tone, setting the expectations, getting started, first steps. It doesn't matter if, like you, this is your first time, or if you've been a leader for twenty years and starting your first day at a new job. The principles are the same as is the timeframe.

Why ninety days? Why not sixty? Why not thirty-seven? No particular reason, other than in my years of experience this is about how long it has taken to do it all the right way. It's certainly possible that if a lot of things line up correctly it can be done in less than ninety days; if you've got a lot of messes to clean up it could take longer. The real key behind the ninety day timeframe is to keep you focused on getting this all done, and getting it all done <u>as quickly as you can without being sloppy</u>. Ninety days will go by incredibly fast, and unless you stay focused too many of these things will slide for too long and you'll not make the strong impression you really need to.

The 10 for 90 is intended as a roadmap, a to-do list, for all the things I've found are the most important to get done to make that first set of impressions as you take over. They are in roughly the order that you should do them in, but by no means are they required to be consecutive. The more of these you can do concurrently the better off you'll be, if for no other reason than you'll get done sooner.

Get the 10 for 90 done, and you will have impressed everyone that even though you're new, you're a solid leader who has clearly taken charge and is poised for great things.

The List: 10 Things to Do in the First 90 Days

1. Assess Yourself & Your Team

Leadership is at its core, equal parts science and art. As you take your new assignment, use the artist metaphor as you step into your new role.

What does an artist do? The first thing any artist does is to check their materials and tools. Does she have all of the materials she'll need to create her painting – does she have all the paints she needs, in the right proportions, in the right colors? Does she have her canvas? Is it prepared properly so that she's ready to go as soon as she picks up a brush? Does she have all the brushes (type, size) she'll need for the type of painting she wants this next one to be?

You need to do the same. If your team/group/department is your canvas, you and your people are the tools of the trade.

Yourself

What are your strengths? Typically, one or more of these is what directly contributed to you having the job you now have. (Yes, I did tell you in earlier chapters that what got you here ain't gonna keep you here. However, there are traits and strengths you have that can be ADAPTED to your new role and will serve you well – so seeming contradiction aside, it is time extremely well-spent to do this self-analysis.) Put yourself in your manager's shoes, and think about what, from their perspective, you think they saw in you. Are you detail-oriented? Are you organized? Do you keep your cool during tough times/crises? Are you good with numbers? Are you good with people? Are you a good communicator?

Take some time to do this. Write them down. Your goal is to put together a dossier about yourself. If you have trouble with this, and most people do, ask a close friend or a colleague to give you some feedback. You might also get some clues from your past performance reviews, or from the promotion announcement that your boss likely distributed to trumpet your new role.

Now do the same with your weaknesses, or "challenges" as the HR people love to say. Write these down too.

You may have done this before; if so this won't take too long. If you haven't, don't worry. This is important, so take all the time you need. Once this is complete, take a look at the list in the context of your new circumstances. What are the strengths that directly relate to being a leader? How do you think you can best leverage each of your skills to jump-start you in your "start-up" phase? What are some gaps between what strong skills you do have with what skills you believe you'll need?

Taking a look at gaps in your strengths is a logical starting point to take a look at your weaknesses. Again, look at these from your boss's perspective, or maybe match up your skills against people you consider good/great leaders. What is it that you aren't so hot at that you think you SHOULD be? What areas are you challenged in that might cause you to underperform? As with the strengths, write them all down.

Now that you have the information, you can start figuring out what to do about it. For the gaps and the actual weaknesses, you have three choices: fix it, compensate for it, or delegate it.

Fix: if for example you've identified that you need to be better at project management you can take classes, get yourself some books on the subject, or find some online communities devoted to the craft.

Compensate: if you can de-emphasize/avoid situations that put you in a position that would cause you to need this skill. For project management in particular this probably won't work, and for the most part compensation is only a short-term solution. You can bet the farm that sooner or later you'll be put in a position where you can't avoid your weakness. Murphy's Law being what it is that time will come sooner or later and the stakes will of course be high. Only use "compensate" as a bridge to one of the other two choices.

Delegate: in some cases someone working for you may have strength in an area you are weak; it may be possible to delegate those kinds of tasks to him or her. In the case of project management, you can make this person your go-to project manager. If you have a strong level of trust with this person this can be a great situation. The only caution here is that if this area (in our example, project management) is a significant weakness for you, it will be difficult to assess, and mentor if necessary, the work you've delegated. Another caveat is that not all tasks can be delegated; some of your tasks (for example, most people tasks) are not appropriate to delegate.

Your Team

Once you've done this for yourself, you need to turn your attention to your team. This part may need to be done concurrently with the task of assessing what your team does to really finish it, but we'll get to that later. The key thing here is to get to know, really know, all your new staff as people. Some managers advocate starting by going to HR and getting their performance evaluations, to see what previous managers have thought of them.

BAD IDEA.

I've never been a fan of looking at HR files first. Why? Several reasons. Maybe the previous bosses were lousy managers. Maybe the other managers had this person misplaced on the team, putting this person in a situation where they were set up to struggle, if not fail outright. Maybe the previous managers couldn't recognize potential in someone if it jumped up and bit them. Or maybe the new teammate is just very, very good at kissing up to management to get high marks on performance appraisals. Most importantly, I like to make up my own mind first without letting other opinions color my judgment. See for yourself. Do your own research. Make your own first conclusions. Then, and only then, go back and look at the HR file. If you find differences between your assessment and the file, use that as a starting point for further investigation.

The best way to get to know these people is (obviously) one-on-one in a more casual setting like lunch. Don't, I repeat don't, do something like this in a conference room if you can possibly avoid it. Why? Because no matter how hard you try it will come off like a police interrogation. It's way too formal, and they'll likely treat it like an interview. If you think lunch with everyone isn't practical, at least get out of your usual area of the building. Get to a break room (as long as it's empty or sparsely populated at the time), or take a walk around the building in nice weather. If you can get them some place more casual, the better you both will feel and, since they'll be more at ease, the more you can find out about them. As best as you can, discover what makes them tick. What are their core beliefs? What is important to them? What are their opinions about work in general and specifically, work in your group? What are their goals and dreams? If they were in your shoes, what would they change? What would they keep?

Two things: one, obviously getting to know someone well and even getting through this short example list of questions, takes a whole lot longer than one conversation at a Starbucks. It might take months. Two, some of this may be better done watching them as they work. (Tell the truth, now – are you ALWAYS as good and righteous and productive as you will say you are in your next interview?) So no, you won't get the full picture right away. But you need to get started, NOW, and as you talk to the rest of your team, the picture will start to come into focus.

As you're talking with them and/or watching them work, ask yourself these questions:

- Does this person seem to be honest?
- Does this person have convictions? What are they? Do they fit with the team and where you think you want to lead it?
- Do they use the word "we" more than the word "I"?
- Do they seem to have a bias for getting things done, or for whining about why it doesn't?
- How good of a fit do they seem in their current role?
- What do they seem to do well? What do they seem to have trouble with?
- What do you think their potential might be? (Key point: NOT just in the role they're in. Think five years from now. With training and mentoring, how might you be able to help them grow?)

- Do you think you'd ever want to promote this person? Would you ever want them to be YOUR boss?
- Do they seem to be one of the "good guys" or one of the "bad actors"? (Don't be too hasty either way here. With some attention and guidance bad actors can become one of your most effective people, and those who initially seem like the best that ever was are just snowing you.

Another good way to get information about your team is to ask around. Ask the other areas and departments that your team regularly deals with. Who have they worked with on your team? What has their experience been dealing with your team? If they could change one thing, what would they want that to be? What things are your team doing well?

People (obviously!) are very complex, so you'll want to assess them in various situations and with various people. Keep this assessment "top of mind" during your first few work days. If you're to build something great you need to know what you're working with. Resist the impulse to change things right away; you're likely to get it wrong. Wait until you get a few more of the 10 for 90 under your belt.

2. Find Out What Your Manager's Expectations Are

Before you get too far, it's critical for you to find out what your boss is expecting of you in your new role. She may have brought you in to shake things up or she may want you to keep things going as they've always been. Whatever your ideas are of where you want to take this team, you need to make sure they line up with your boss. Things to ask:

- Are there issues to resolve? In what areas – personnel, process, quality, inter-group relations, productivity?
- What's important to her?
- How does she want you to communicate with her? Some people prefer one-on-one verbal communication; some prefer written status-type reports. Do they prefer email? IM? Phone? What's the frequency of communication she's looking for; once a day, once a week? (If she's a good manager she'll likely want pretty frequent chats early on to make sure you're getting started on the right foot – and to see how you're adapting to your new role. Basically she's trying to find out how well you're doing).
- What are your boss's goals for her area, and how does she see your team contributing to that?

Finally, you need to know what she thinks are YOUR top three goals for your first ninety days. What would you have to get done for her to consider your first three months on the job a success? Interestingly, she may not have thought of this before, in which case it's a great thing for you to have prodded her into considering it. At the end of this conversation, BOTH of you should have a clear idea of what you have to do in order for both of you to proclaim your first ninety days as a success.

3. Assess the Culture of the Team (And the Larger Organization)

We're stepping into some murky, squishy stuff here, but bear with me. It'll be worth it.

What is the culture of your team? Culture is a big word, and many managers don't address it at all because they tend to think that "culture" is something that is a corporate-level thing, not a team/department thing. Well, thinking that way is HALF right. There is most definitely a corporate culture, and we'll touch on that in a bit – because you'll need to know that as well. (For example, if your team is part of a large, buttoned-down accounting firm chock-full of overly-thick carpeting, opulent cherry-wood furniture and expensive wingtips on the feet of every male manager, you'll have a difficult time remaking your team as a group of swashbucklers willing to take on authority. (It can be done; but you better know what you're up against going in!)

To assess your team's culture, you will be looking to find out about these four things:

- Beliefs
- Values
- Rituals
- Stories

These four things weave together the fabric of your team and makes them "what they are".

To find out about beliefs, dig out the answers to these questions: What are their beliefs about themselves? Do they think of themselves as important cogs in the company wheel? Do they believe they are "intrapreneurs", that is employees doing entrepreneurial stuff? Do they feel valued, or do they feel like ants in the anthill of (corporate) life, or as company rebels? What are their beliefs about how their team fits in the organization? Do they feel the group is integral to the bigger picture, or do they feel like they're living in some company backwater?

As for values, what is important to them as a team? What is "good" behavior in their eyes, and what is "bad"? Do they value and encourage debate, or is that viewed as disrespectful? Are they an "in by 8 a.m. out by 5 p.m." group, or more of a "come in whenever the hell you want as long as you get your job done on time" crowd? (I once was a part of a team that if I got in to work by 7:10 a.m. I was the last guy in, facing some nasty, "well look who FINALLY strolled in" stares). Do they value and encourage fun in the workplace? Do they value teamwork or personal initiative? Do they get together for after-work activities or go their own separate ways when the 5 p.m. whistle blows?

Next up, rituals. What are your team's rituals? These can be formal, like a Team Member of the Month award, or informal, like a Friday afternoon Social Club at the local watering hole, or Doughnut Day. What do they celebrate, and how do they do it?

Last but certainly(!) not least, stories. Stories are the transmission vehicle, the thread that weaves the fabric of the culture together. It highlights and celebrates what makes the team unique. It tells the tales of victory and success, the times of failure, the incidents where all looked bleak and the team rallied to get the job done. It also might tell the story of when Mr. Big (literally) got a pie in the face at the company picnic. As you speak with your team, ask questions that will draw out the stories and the storytelling. Pay attention to two things:

the content and tone of the stories, and the emotions they elicit from the storyteller and those hearing it. Are the stories uplifting, fun or depressing? What is being viewed as "legendary" in these stories? Is it that so-and-so worked a zillion overtime hours? Was it an act of kindness? Was it a special act of teamwork, like in the movie "Officer and a Gentleman" when Richard Gere's character is running an obstacle course, but stops and gives up his chance to get a (much-needed) lowest time in order to encourage one of his teammates to get over a wall they've never been able to get over? Or are the stories more of death-marches, or someone yelling at someone else? As the stories are told, how is everyone else reacting? Upbeat or downcast? Enthused or cynical?

Listen closely to the stories and their (re)telling. You can find out more in a twenty minute story session than in weeks of conversation.

Why is all this important?

Cultures are very powerful. Cultures govern almost everything that happens inside a team. Cultures explain, for the most part, why the team does what it does on a minute-by-minute basis. As you talk to everyone, as you watch them operate, you will begin to make your judgments about what you want to do: what you want to keep, what you want to tweak, what you want to blow up. As you make those plans you need to determine if your changes are consistent with the current culture or not. If not, be advised your job is bigger than just tweaking a process; you're going at the core of who the team is. Now maybe that's exactly what's needed. A sloppy, unfocused, underperforming team (for whatever reason) has a culture that tolerates sloppiness and "just getting by". Clearly, the team I describe needs a culture change. But it is more difficult and takes longer, so prepare yourself. And certainly check this with your boss, to make sure your ideas match up with hers.

Most importantly, to change the core of a team you need to start at the core. You need to change, or sometimes just remind them of, the REASONS they should be making the change you want them to. Why does this team exist? Why should they all get out of bed in the morning to come to work? What is important and special about the work? More on this in #9 and #10 in the 10 for 90.

4. Who Are Your Clients? Your Customers?

On a day-to-day basis who does your team interact with? Who are your clients, that is, who are the people and groups inside the organization that depend on your work? If applicable, who are your customers, that is, people outside the organization receiving your output? Depending on what your team does, you may have both or you may just have one. An IT department, for example, typically only has internal clients; although the web services team certainly also has customers – everyone on the Internet that uses the organization's public website.

A good place to start is to make a list of both. You can begin by just writing down the groups that use what your team produces, like Accounting, IT, Sales. Do the same with your customers if you can: the IT department at Acme Trucking, the Printing department of Joe's Printing, etc. Once you're done, go back and look again. Many times there are things your team does for others that no one remembers. Keep in mind that sometimes, though, that web-page you populate every day with the XYZ report isn't even used anymore, so it would probably be a good idea to stop producing it! More on this in #5, 6, 7, and 8 of the 10 for 90.

Was that tough? Many times this exercise ends up being harder than anyone might think. But it's well worth it, as there's nothing more important than knowing who you're supposed to be keeping happy.

Now take that list of groups and go one level deeper: WHO are the people in those groups you deal with routinely? If at this point you only know the people by their functional titles (Assistant Comptroller, Web Services Security Admin) that's fine for now, but the ultimate goal here is to find out the real people who utilize your workplace.

The reason for all this work is simple. So simple, in fact, that most leaders don't think to do this EVER. But it's so simple and so powerful. If you know who those people are, you can seek them out and begin to build a relationship with them. And, in your position as new leader, you'll want to talk to these people to get a sense from outside your group as to how well your team has been doing from THEIR perspective. Especially as a brand-new leader, you'll have no skin in the game and they will be more likely to tell you what they really feel.

Remember as you talk to them, though, to not make any hasty promises you may not be able to keep later. As with your one-on-ones with your team, stay in "information gathering" mode and stay out of "problem-solving" mode - at least for now.

Find out who your clients are, who your customers are and contact them. Take them to lunch if you can. Valuable insights about your team from an objective perspective are there for the asking.

5. What Does Your Team Do, *Really?*

You've talked with your team. You've watched them in action. You've chatted with your clients. By now you should have a sense of what your team does: "We provide sales support to our outside sales group" or "We provide system administration for all the servers in the XYZ Division."

But as with your list of clients/customers, take another look and go a little deeper. Very often, over the years all sorts of tasks end up getting done that your group really shouldn't be doing. As an example, I took over a team that had its own database administrator (DBA) since our team dealt with a lot of data files that came in from clients, got processed by us, and then massaged into a series of performance reports. I thought I knew exactly what our team and the DBA did, but during the first several weeks I kept hearing from the DBA how busy he was and that some of his project work would have to wait. This quickly became problematic (go figure!) so I sat down to have a talk with him about it. It turned out that since our team (and the DBA in particular) was sitting on a mountain of client information, all sorts of people inside the company would ask him for data extracts, reports, and all sorts of other stuff. As I quizzed my DBA it became apparent that this kind of ad-hoc work was taking up a good 20-25 hours a week. No WONDER he wasn't ever getting any project work done! More on this example later, but that's why you need to dig deep "under the covers" to find out what your team is REALLY doing.

The next thing to do is to take this question and turn it on its head. You now know what you ARE doing, but what COULD you be doing to make you and your team more responsive and more valuable to your clients/customers? There's an oft-repeated management nugget that talks about the U.S. transportation industry immediately prior to the introduction of the automobile in the late 1890s and early 1900s. As the story goes, there were a number of companies that were in the business of making buggy whips for horse-drawn carriages. When autos were introduced, any company solely devoted to buggy-whip manufacturing quickly went out of business. The moral of this story is one of perspective and vision: if the buggy-whip makers had thought of themselves as being in the "vehicle acceleration" business, instead of the much(!) more limiting "buggy-whip making" business, some of them at least would've found a way to transition from buggy-whips to, oh I don't know, fuel pumps or accelerator-pedal linkages. They would have made the transition from one technology to the next if they'd had a broader vision of their company's job was.

My point: Look at what you're doing, all of it, and see how you can change it, alter it, expand upon it to deliver more value to your clients. (All those conversations you just had with your clients and customers are looking even more valuable now, eh? All that juicy info on what they need relative to your team...)

As a leader, you're in the potential business, not just for your people, but for your team as well.

6. How Does Your Team Do What They Do?

Okay, so you've now got a sense of what your team does and have started to explore some of the "hidden' things they do as well as an inkling of what they might be capable of doing.

But HOW do they do it? This is where we start looking at process. In many cases, process trumps people. I've been in a number of situations where I saw that really good people were underperforming because the process they were working in did not allow them to succeed, or to perform at a high level. In fact the process fought them at every turn. As you look at your new team, how are the processes?

Remember my example of my DBA? Well, the process that had evolved in that team was one where the DBA took all sorts of data requests in a very ad-hoc manner; he was getting work just by walking through the halls. People would stop him and say, "Hey, Bill, can you get me some data on XYZ Bank? I have a presentation on Thursday and really need..." In this case, the process of work intake was completely unorganized and had not control of the timelines. Could Bill really get that request done by Thursday? What about the four other requests he might get in similar fashion on the way back to his desk? And oh, by the way, what about his "scheduled" work, the work I thought at first was the only work he was doing?

In this particular case, I sent out an email to the "usual suspects" that hit Bill up for work, telling them that Bill had a number of key tasks he had to do and that he could no longer take work requests the old way. I told them that while we would be glad to continue to accommodate their requests, any request had to come through me so it could be scheduled in with the rest of our (and Bill's) work. Knowing full well that this email would likely not stop everyone from trying to "sneak one past me", I told Bill specifically that if anyone asked him for work directly he was empowered to tell them that the only way he could work on it was if they asked me. By changing the process this way I not only gained much greater control of what was on Bill's plate, I reduced his stress immeasurably and also preserved all his relationships with his colleagues: HE wasn't the bad guy saying "no", I was.

This is a small example, but illustrates well that correct process drives good productivity. If I'd let the old way continue, Bill would've ended up working harder and harder to keep up with the ad-hoc requests while I kept getting on his case about the (scheduled) project work. Inevitably, Bill would've fallen behind and both he and our team would've gotten a reputation of not being able to deliver.

Another informative example of how important process is in governing productivity, I give you the Red Bead Experiment, made famous by W. Edwards Deming.[2]

Deming, often called the Father of Quality, helped Japan's manufacturing sector pull itself out of the destruction of World War II to become a worldwide economic force by following Deming's principles. Deming's work finally got the attention it deserved in the U.S. in the 1980s. When he would give lectures and seminars he often would conduct an experiment which involved bringing three people on-stage out of the audience and telling them they were to be "employees" working for him in his "factory". He gave them all wooden paddles with many little indentations on them. He then would lead them one-by-one to a barrel full of mostly white marbles or beads, with some red ones. The "job" of each "employee" was to dip their paddles into the barrel with the objective of pulling out as many red beads as possible. If the first person (almost invariably) would pull out few red beads, Deming would chastise them for not being productive enough. If the next "employee" pulled out more (of course, entirely by chance) Deming would congratulate them and tell the first "employee" that they might want to work harder to be more like "employee" #2.

The experiment would go on until Deming had hammered home the fact that in many organizations there are processes like this (perhaps not purely as random as the experiment is set up) that no matter how hard the employees work they don't control the output as much as the process does.

Keep this at the top-of-you-mind as you look at, and consider modifying, your team's processes. What is working, REALLY? Are your processes helping your team or are they fighting them? What would make things better?

7. **How WELL Do They Do What They Do?**

In 2002, Larry Bossidy, the former high-level executive at General Electric and later CEO of Honeywell, co-authored a book titled "Execution: The Discipline of Getting Things Done". It is an excellent book for you to get into the nitty-gritty details of building and implementing processes that enhance your team's ability to get things accomplished well time after time. It's a great book for you to delve deep into the concept of processes; Bossidy goes into significant detail about why execution is important, the building blocks, and how to tie together people, strategy, and operational aspects to make it all work effectively. I highly recommend the book.[1]

Bossidy's work is very detailed and may be too much information as you're getting started. This is an area that you can postpone a bit in terms of getting highly schooled on all the nuances of process. For now, just keep in mind the lessons of the Red Bead Experiment that process can either drive, or limit, productivity.

Always remember that your team's value is driven not only by the ability to get things done, but to get it done WELL, EVERY time.

8. **Why Does Your Team Do What They Do? Does Anyone Even *Know?***

This is probably the most under-asked question out there. I would venture to say that if you walked up to one hundred different leaders and asked them this question you would be guaranteed to receive at least ninety-nine blank stares. Maybe even a hundred. How about you? Did YOU give me a blank stare and secretly wonder if I'd lost my mind?

Well, I'm happy to say I haven't, and neither have you. In today's environment, with technology facilitating sub-second everything and a fascination with the delivery mechanism ("I just GOTTA have that new iPhone!") we have gotten ourselves to a point where we don't ask "why" anymore. We will ask "how", we will ask "what", but almost never ask "why". After all it is what it is, right?

But we do ourselves, our organizations, and our ability to lead a great disservice by neglecting "why". "Why" is the most powerful concept we have as leaders; it's the basis for how we, as leaders, get ANYONE to follow us. Much more on this in #9 and #10 on the 10 for 90 list; for now I'll limit the discussion to your team itself.

Your team does stuff every day. My DBA dealt with data all day, analyzing, processing, defining, storing, and maintaining structures for efficient storage and easy retrieval. But why? If you're in HR, you work to put together company events, or the latest employee survey, or analyze the latest EEOC regulation. *Why?*

Answering "well, that's our job" doesn't cut it; it's a circular reference. I want you to elevate your thinking, broaden it. The purpose of this item on the List, as well as #9 and #10 are to help you put together a *raison d'etre,* literally translated as "a reason to be".

Ask the third baseman for the Minnesota Twins why he fields grounders in a game and throws the ball to first. He might say,

"To get the runner out". But if you push him a bit, and say "No, WHY do you do that?" he'll get your meaning and say, "To win this game so we can win more games and eventually win the World Series." THAT's the "why" that gets him to the ballpark early, the "why" that makes him take an extra hour of batting practice, the "why" that makes him play with injury.

This is the "why" I want you to be looking for with YOUR team. Yes, your group has a specific function, just as the third base-man does. But look to determine how that function can translate into a statement of "why" that is more compelling. What is your "World Series"?

Go back to my example with Bill the DBA. That team, when I took it over, had terrible morale and no "why". That team managed all the data and back-end systems that, in effect, were the center of what the company did. However, there was also another small group that worked on a software application that utilized the data which we sold to our clients. That app was a major cash-cow for the company, and the people on it were given a status that (for that smallish company anyway) approached rock-star status.

I needed to find a way to give them a compelling "why". As I analyzed what our group did, it became clear to me that not only was my group NOT the corporate backwater my new team thought it was, it was indeed the engine of everything the company did. Even the sexy software app needed the data my group created.

At first no one on my team bought the "we are the shepherds of the data that drives everything this company does" mantra

I was preaching, but as soon as they saw that I was (very) sincere and I could show them concrete examples of what I meant, they started to come on board. They wanted to be a part of something bigger, something better, something they could be proud of and the new team "why" was exactly what they needed.

In #9 and #10 I'll expand on how this all played out. But order is important here. Once I had my "World Series", my (compelling) vision of why we were doing what we were doing, it gave them something to believe in and a reason to follow me.

9. **The Strategy Thing, Or How the "Why" Actually Happens**

If you've done #8 right, you've now got your new team starting to buy in, starting to want to follow your lead. But that enthusiasm can fade quickly if it's not backed by something concrete to actually deliver on the "why" you've outlined. If you've ever attended a seminar by a motivational speaker you likely know what I mean. Most of them do a GREAT job getting you fired up and feeling good, but almost none of them give you any practical advice or roadmap for actually doing anything with what you've just learned. Without translating the feelings into action, there is no progress and three days after the seminar you are right back where you started from.

What you need now is a strategy, which is just a fancy way of saying "you need a plan, Stan." (Sorry). If your little team's "why" is that you do X for the organization, how do you/or will you show it? This is especially necessary if your vision of your group's "why" is bigger than it has been before. Your group needs to know how you think they're gonna get there.

10. Build a Plan to Inspire Them

If you've done planning before this is all old hat to you. But if you haven't, here are some brief tips. There are hundreds of books and other resources on project planning out there which can give you a much more detailed presentation of the topic than I can here. But initially, at least, you don't have to get that detailed. In fact, it'll be better if you don't. Let me use a metaphor to illustrate my point: let's say your 'why" involved taking your whole team on a cross-country trip. How would you plan to get them there?

Start by breaking all of the details into logical "chunks". Don't EVER try to plan everything at once; your head will explode. For a cross-country trip, your chunks might be:

- Specify destination
- Specify departure point
- Determine mode of transportation
- Determine departure date
- Determine length of say, if applicable
- Determine food & lodging arrangements

Since this is very high level, you'll need to go another level down detail-wise to make this more real to your team. Your initial presentation to the team would be something like, "Okay, gang, we've already discussed the need for us to go to the West Coast. Based on my research I believe we need to proceed to Salem, Oregon for a period of three weeks. Since time is more of the essence than cost, the best way for us to get there is by air. We'll need to leave sometime between the 16th and the 22nd of next month; I'm thinking we'll depart from Westchester because the logistics are much easier than at LaGuardia. Doing this will help us better achieve our core purpose of..."

As you can see, there are a million details still unanswered at this point. But at this point it doesn't matter. You've started with a vision of "why", and now you've laid out how it can be achieved; you've made it specific in time and place. Your team now has something real to hang on to, something to give them the sense that this is ACTUALLY going to happen. Which generates a whole new level of enthusiasm that makes your team even stronger. And all those details still left to be planned out? They're a perfect vehicle for getting your team aligned with the plan – let them (if appropriate) work out the rest of the details! Is there a budding project manager on your team? Let them take the lead. Is there someone on your team who loves finding the best hotel for the money anywhere they go? Give that task to them.

By doing all this, you've given your new "why" substance. It's not just a nice little idea anymore, you've begun to make it real with a pathway to get there. By involving the team in the detail aspects of the planning where appropriate, you're allowing them to "wear" the plan as their own. Now it's not YOUR plan, it's THEIR plan. And their feelings of contribution, morale, and pride will likely be off the charts compared to what it was just a short time ago.

...

Now that you've got them this far, your job becomes three-fold. The first two are working the plan you and your team have put together, making sure as time goes on that you keep adding new steps or new sub-plans to the plan. NEVER leave a goal hanging out there with nothing planned after it; this can be disastrous. There have been several instances where Olympic athletes have worked for years to get that gold medal, and then when they do they're completely depressed because they never stopped to think about what they would do after the medal ceremony. Don't let his happen to your team. Always have a second act, a third, and a...) The third thing you'll have to work on is to keep the "why" alive, to keep it in full view, to show your team how their day-to-day, week-to-week accomplishments on the plan is fulfilling their "why".

This is key (VERY).

What can commonly happen is that as you succeed, the tendency is to get so wrapped up in the succeeding that you tend to forget the "why" of your organization. Or as your group grows, the translation of the "why" to the new members starts to get a little fuzzy. This is why, as we discussed in #8, you get blank stares when you ask people why they do what they do or why their team does what it does. Simon Sinek, the author of *Start with Why: How Great Leaders Inspire Everyone to Take Action* talks about the split that occurs when a group or organization starts losing its connection with its "why", and none of it is good.[3,4]

Recap & T.T.R.

- Your first ninety days probably can't make you and your new leadership role, but they certainly can break you. Use this 10 for 90 as a blueprint to avoid false starts and slingshot your way to a great new phase to your career.
- Know your people, inside and out. They, and how they perform, are how you will be judged. You will succeed or fail through them.
- Understand your manager's expectations of you.
- Understand the environment your team works in: the culture and the relationships it has with clients, customers, and colleagues.
- Figure out what your team does; find any "hidden" work.
- Understand the power of process to drive or hinder productivity; remember the Red Bead Experiment!
- Determine what your team's "why" is and should be.
- Make it real by creating a plan to make it happen. Get everyone involved.
- Avoid what Simon Sinek calls 'the split"; make sure you keep your team closely connected to how their ongoing progress is the realization of their "why". Keep them inspired!

Chapter Notes

[1]Pick up "Execution: The Discipline of Getting Things Done" by Larry Bossidy and Ram Charan at Amazon.com -- http://

www.amazon.com/Execution-Discipline-Getting-Things-Done/ dp/0609610570/ref=sr_1_1?s=books&ie=UTF8&qid=1326671576& sr=1-1

[2]Go to Google and just do a search on "Deming red bead experiment"; you'll find a number of hits for both text and video descriptions of the full experiment.

[3]Simon Sinek, *Start with Why: How Great Leaders Inspire Everyone to Take Action*, The Penguin Group, 2009, Chapter 12, "Split Happens".

[4]Video from Sinek's website, www.startwithwhy.com: http://www. startwithwhy.com/Learn/LearningLibrary.aspx?control=ViewGal leryPhotos&HideLink=1&GalleryID=10&photoID The description of "split" starts about two and a half minutes into the video…

CHAPTER 6

TRUST, UNITY, & PERFORMANCE

People who work together will win, whether it be against complex football defenses, or the problems of modern society.

— *Vince Lombardi*

Actually, this topic could've easily been #11 in the "11 for 90", but I've broken it out due to its importance.

This is the one item, the one characteristic of a group or organization, that will make it a truly well-oiled unit and opens the door to greatness. Without it, you can master EVERYTHING else in this book and not really get anywhere. You'll end up sitting at your desk wondering why all your efforts don't seem to work.
In actuality, trust is the foundation of any real effort to make a difference. If you can get a group to trust, all sorts of specific good things happen:

- Trust cements the commitment to the "why" and each other
- This makes everyone engaged to a high degree and has them coming to work every day ready to "rock 'n roll"; performance levels will be (much!) higher
    - Much faster execution with fewer mistakes
- Fewer nasty surprises; the ability of everyone to ask the tough questions means fewer problems that are allowed to lurk
- Much increased sense of group pride and ownership
- Much improved sense of team loyalty and belonging; it can feel almost like family (in a GOOD way!)
    - Team gets a reputation of being high performers, which enhances everyone's career prospects

Sounds great, doesn't it? It should. If you've ever been on a team with real trust going for it, you still remember it fondly, don't you? You probably remember everyone's names, their funny personality quirks, their strengths, and at least one "war story" per person and all the memorable accomplishments. Whether it was last week or ten years ago you <u>remember</u>. With pride. And maybe nostalgia, because you've not experienced that again.

Your gut, and your experience, tell you that this kind of trust (and accomplishment) is rare. And your gut would be right. But it doesn't have to be. You, as a leader, can <u>create</u> this environment within your team/group; be advised there are no shortcuts but it can be done if you're committed. And as I've shown (and your gut tells you) the results can be truly special.

So how is that done? How is trust built?

First, let's get a little more detailed about what exactly trust is in the context of a team, a group, and organization.

Trust is more than just "I got your back"; it's a feeling people and groups have for one another when the following conditions exist between all parties:

Long-term track record

What do we know about each other that we take to be true? How have each of us acted over the long haul? What have we all done in this situation before and can we count on each other to do it again? Yes, I may have been in a situation where I raised overall sales by 20% in six months, but do you <u>trust</u> that I can do that again, now, when we need it? Have I done it just the one time, or have I done it again and again? This is what "track record" means; and it breaks down into the following categories:

- **Even tempered** – how do you handle day-to-day situations? How do you handle the stressful ones? Is your track record one of being rock solid and positive no matter what the situation, or are you fine until the going gets tough and then you get negative or freak out/lose it?

- **Consistent** – is your performance consistent over time or all over the place? Somebody who is not a great performer but can always be counted on to hit about 75% of the goal may be more trustable than someone who can hit 120% of goal one month and 50% of goal the next. Note here that either person in this example is not necessarily good or bad. There's a lot less upside with "Ms. 75%", but if you need that 75% you'll sleep a lot better than if you have "Mr. Erratic" on your team. But if you're in a situation where you need a big month, "Mr. Erratic" might be the better bet, but not many of you will be comfortable about it.

- **Commitment to the group** - A down-in-your-bones feeling among all that, at the end of the day, we are all "for" each other...That means no hidden agendas, no disguised hurts, no axes to grind, no festering jealousies. Period.

- **Commitment to honesty with compassion** – this is easier to say than to do, but everyone has to buy into this and be willing to commit a bit of themselves, be a little bit vulnerable, and agree to be able to: 1) Say what needs to be said even if it feels uncomfortable; 2) Hear what needs to be heard; and 3) Use compassion without sugar-coating.

- The point is to get to the (sometimes hard) truths that will keep you from succeeding if left unsaid and unheard. And to do it in a way that points up the problem to be solved, NOT to place blame or demean anyone. This is something that gets better with practice if everyone truly is thinking first an foremost of what's best for the group as a whole, both now and in the future. Burning someone down now to get at the problem ("Fred, I told you it would be a stupid idea to do that but you went ahead anyway!!!") may get today's problem solved but you'll probably never get any of Fred's buy-in on anything for the team (or certainly you) again. Short term gain, long term pain.

- **Ownership** – a feeling pervasive within the group that this is OUR team, OUR project. It's not the bosses giving us work to do, it's something WE are committed to doing and doing right. If everyone believes that have a true ownership role they will make smarter/better/faster/higher quality decisions.

Short term via a team "compact"

This concept actually may seem counterintuitive, and maybe even a tad legalistic. "Geez, Paul, you mean we're going to get together and write a contract to play nice with each other? What's next; are you going to make us pinky-swear?" (Such sarcasm from you guys!) The short answer: Hey, if a pinky-swear is what it takes go for it. (Sarcasm right back at ya!)

But seriously, why not? Why not sit down and work all this out ahead of time, before it's needed, before crunch time hits and the pressure's on? Work this out together, get explicit. The vibe should be one of "WE define what trust means to us", and "WE define what we'll do (actions we'll take) to make it real". Just the exercise alone is a great team building effort; you get a chance to sit down as a team and define what is truly important to the group. And how you'll all make it work, and how you'll all be accountable for it.

How to Make it Happen

Get the team together. Get them together offsite if you can (this is be best but may not be logistically practical). You want them focused on nothing but this. If you can't get them offsite, at least book a room well away from your usual haunts – a conference room on a different floor, in a different building. Make the meeting time at least 2 hours; you want time to spend thinking deeply about this topic and time to muscle through the inevitable sticking points. Turn off the phones. Talk through each of these in depth and come to real agreement, not polite (but false) consensus.

- Do we have a "why"?
  - Why does our group exist? What does it REALLY do? What do we WANT it to do and be known for? What is it about why we do what we do that is important? Does our "why" make us want to come in to work at 3 in the morning in the crappiest weather imaginable? (If not, you haven't found your real "why" yet. Keep looking.)

- What's been our history? Good? Bad?
  First things first; take the time as a group to determine your tendencies over the past few years. Many times just taking the time to step back a bit and look at what and how you've been doing things is constructive.
  If you're a newly-formed team, or a team that has had substantial personnel change, you won't need to spend much time here. Just jump ahead to talking about how you as a group WANT things to be.

- ○ Question to ask: What made the bad times bad and the good times good?
  - ▪ Describe a couple of your biggest successes. What specific actions did your group take to make it a success? Did they take a bold risk? Did they avoid a big problem? How did you do it?
  - ▪ Describe a couple of your biggest stumbles. Analyze it with some of the same questions you asked for the good results.
  - ▪ Document the results on a whiteboard or flip chart; something big that everyone in the room can see. From the lists, can your group identify major themes or recurring patterns? For example, do you seem to be overly consensus-driven as a group? Do you seem to be lacking in a certain skill/knowledge area? Do you seem to be great at, say, logistics? Once you have this done, it will be much easier for you all to see the gaps in what your group knows/does and what you need to know/do.

- What do we want to keep/toss?
  Now that you've identified all these items and the gaps, you can identify which of those characteristics you want to keep and enhance, and which ones you need to eliminate (or at least minimize). With any particular gap, you can attack it either "globally", that is by eliminating the gap in everyone, or "tactically", by perhaps picking a group "expert" to drive any activities in that area. For example, a "global" gap fix might be to make sure everyone in the group takes communications training to improve information flow through the group, and a "tactical" gap fix might be to assign Fred

to be your planner because Fred is better at it than anyone else. If planning has been a problem, as best you can make Fred the planning guru. And over time he can even train the rest of you to make the gap fix more "global" over time.

- What's the end game? What do we want to look like when we're done?
  This is where you build the "new you", the new way of working for your group. Of all your identified gaps and strengths, how do you as a group WANT to be? How do you want to interact? How do you want to support each other? How would your group operate during its "best day ever"?

- How will we all be accountable to making this happen? How will the group "self-manage" the process and keep people doing their part?
- Document the Common Purpose
  Boil down all of the learning you've done into a concise, simple description of

  - What we do
  - Why we do it
  - How we commit to each other
    - What attitudes
    - What behaviors
    - How we will be accountable to each other so we all take ownership

And then I recommend all of you, one by one, commit to the document and commit to the group. If someone can't commit you're not there yet.

This exercise won't always be smooth and simple; but if you can do this you are MILES further along than most any other team/group out there. And you'll be in a place where everyone knows what everyone is committed to doing, and therefore can TRUST EACH OTHER.

Congratulations; your group is on the threshold of being one of those special groups you'll all remember fondly years from now. Strap in; it'll be a great ride!

Recap & T.T.R.

- Trust is the foundation of team unity and is the one item, the one characteristic of a group or organization, that will make it a truly well-oiled unit and opens the door to greatness. Without it, you can master EVERYTHING else in this book and not really get anywhere. You'll end up sitting at your desk wondering why all your efforts don't seem to work. Trust is the foundation of any real effort to make a difference.

- The growth of trust within any group doesn't not have to be left to chance; it can be created and managed by creating a team "compact", and agreement of what each member will do for each other member based on the group's values.

CHAPTER 7

BEYOND THE 10 FOR 90

OR HOW TO ACTUALLY CHANGE THE WORLD

The greatest danger for most of us
Is not that our aim is too high and we miss it,
But that it is too low and we achieve it.

— Michelangelo

First Your Team, Then Your Department, Then...

Why do I have this fascination with changing the world, and more specifically with YOU changing the world?

Hark back to the first chapter of this book. It is my fervent belief that the world ABSOLUTELY needs changing, especially the business world. Starting at the top, people are treated more and more like bargaining chips used to balance the books. Lower-level managers set up environments where people are used as cogs in a wheel, transacting only within the small bounds of their codified task - check your brains at the door, please.

I've seen this pattern emerge over the last twenty-five years and have seen all the carnage it has created; I can't watch it continue any more. The way to change it is through new leaders like you who can get on board and create a whole new generation of leaders committed to being the type that gets spectacular results THROUGH people, not by EXPLOITING them. Together we can start to replace the current way of doing business with a much more humane, more inspiring way. A way that alters how the world works – for the better.

The 10 for 90 will give you a fast start down the right road. But in this chapter I'll give you some more actionable hints and tips to really power you toward being a great leader. So start small. Make your team a great team following the roadmap we've already gone through. See what works, what doesn't, and what people respond to. As you grow your own leaders, train THEM in these principles so that as you get promoted to that next level you already have a group of leaders with you that are already true believers. The more of them you can train, the faster the whole organization can benefit by growing closer to a leadership model that makes people excited about the work and can't wait to get at it. If you're REALLY good, "Thank God It's Friday" might just become "Thank God It's Monday".

Build a future of better leaders, one person at a time, and just keep on keepin' on.

Things Great Leaders Do That Bad Ones Don't

1. They Have a "Why"

We've already covered this in #8, #9, and #10 of the 10 for 90. Bad leaders think of themselves, or they think of their people as transactors, or people just on the verge of screwing up at any moment who need to be controlled. Great leaders have both a sense of their own "why" and also one for their team's. They articulate it every chance they get to keep it front and center so that everyone can remember, buy in, and be inspired. Having a "why" gives the team a soul.

2. They Care About People

This too is a bit of a review of what we've chatted about earlier. People are not just important, they are everything. Lee Iacocca, former chairman of Chrysler, was asked once about his managers and their people skills. He reportedly said, "I hate to read in some manager's evaluation that 'he's not good with people.' We don't have any dogs here, no apes – only people." People have an almost unlimited reserve of discretionary effort that they can give you but they'll only give it if they WANT to. A great leader will create an environment of respect and trust that makes them want to give that to you and your team. The results can be amazing.

3. **They Focus on Results**

Great leaders, for the most part, worry about results over anything else. They'd rather accomplish something and have it be a bit messy around the edges than have a beautiful status report written in the most precise language outlining the five reasons the task didn't get done. Obviously, there are professions and tasks (like brain surgery, contract law, or police work) where a sloppy result may not be tolerated. But in too many cases tasks are over thought, over planned, over managed, and under-delivered.

> **"Expect Nothing.**
> **Blame No One.**
> **Do Something!"**
> **— Bill Parcells, former NFL coach**

> **"A good plan executed today is better than a**
> **perfect plan executed at some indefinite point in**
> **the future."**
> **— General George S. Patton Jr.**

As you become a new leader, follow the example of these two men. Always maintain a bias for action. Find a way, even if you or your team are stuck, to keep moving forward. Even if it's a small thing, do it anyway. Accomplishment generates its own momentum, and sometimes momentum itself is enough to get past your issue.

4. **They GTHOOTO! and MBWA**

If you had to remember only two things from this book, these two acronyms might just be your best bet. They are the essence of a people-centric, high-touch, involved leader.

The first, GTHOOTO, was coined by management expert Tom Peters, and it stands for Get The Hell Out Of The Office! As a leader, the absolute WORST thing you can do is hang around in your office reading email, status reports, or executive white-papers. You may think you can effectively lead this way; though it IS possible to lead like this, it is most certainly true that you cannot lead EFFECTIVELY this way. If you stay in your office/cubicle you are (way) too disconnected to what's really happening. At the very least you'll most likely get any information too late to do anything about it while it's happening, so even if you have the best of intentions any response will be too late to do any good.

GTHOOTO's kissin' cousin is MBWA. MBWA was coined by David Packard, the co-founder of Hewlett Packard and stands for Managing By Wandering Around. He advocated and practiced this style of management, where he was a fixture out on the floor amongst his employees. He would stroll around the facilities, asking people questions, helping them solve problems, cleaning roadblocks, <u>all in real time</u>. No time was lost writing (back in that day) a memo to their boss, who might rewrite it to send to Mr. Packard, who then may have gotten it a day or two (or a week) later. And in many cases roadblocks experienced by employees got immediate attention when it was David Packard asking the questions.

How this can work for you is embodied in a somewhat metaphorical sailing example that involved a friend of mine (I'll call him Joe) one summer on Lake Michigan. Joe was a volunteer member of a sailing crew participating in the annual Chicago-to-Mackinac race. This is a race of over 300 vessels sporting over 3,000 crew members. The sailboats are divided into numerous categories by size, design, etc. so that you can compete with other boats of the same configuration. The race, as the name implies, starts at Chicago's Navy Pier and ends at Mackinac Island, 333 statute miles away at the very tippy-top of Lake Michigan.

Joe's sailboat had just undergone a major retrofit that past year and had a bevy of new instruments that captured damn near everything: wind speed, speed of the water current and direction, net speed, and so on. The captain gave everyone a short training lesson on how to read the new instrumentation, and several of the crew were given tasks to watch the instruments and make sure the readouts stayed within a certain range and to report it whenever the readings moved out of the range(s).

Things proceeded well for a time, although they were somewhere in the bottom third of their class. That night, a storm blew in and at one point a bolt of lightning struck their mast. Immediately the voltage fried all of their snazzy new electronics and they were essentially blind. They used their emergency radio to call the Coast Guard, and a quick inspection of the ship revealed the only physical damage appeared to be a hole the size of a quarter in the top gunwale, well above the water line. With the Coast Guard sticking close by to make sure, the captain and crew decided to keep going. All they had to navigate was a sextant, maps, and their knowledge of the route, which they all knew well. Joe recalled that the only way they could gauge how well they were doing was by listening to the sound of this wind, ship, and water, and by observing their movement against stationary objects on shore. Interestingly, over the course of that evening they passed **eight boats in their class**, all of them outfitted with most if not all of the high-end instruments Joe's boat had before the lighting took them all out.

The connection? Managing the sailboat by instruments alone is akin to attempting to manage your team by sitting in your office reading status reports. All the high-tech instruments in the world are no match for being out there, on the floor, watching, listening, and feeling the vibe of what's going on.

Be like David Packard. Wander around and stay (incredibly) in touch with all that's going on, and help your folks cut through all the B.S. They'll love you for it, and you'll know a whole lot more about what's going on than by reading a status report.

Recap & T.T.R.

- Again, the Power of Why
- People, People. People
- Results "R" Us
- Get out there! Wander around!

SECTION 3:

GO!!

CHAPTER 8

A BIT OF COLD WATER

ALL OF THIS IN THE REAL WORLD

I come from an environment where, if you see a snake, you kill it. At GM, if you see a snake, the first thing you do is go hire a consultant on snakes. Then you get a committee on snakes, and then you discuss it for a couple of years. The most likely course of action is -- nothing. You figure, the snake hasn't bitten anybody yet, so you just let him crawl around on the factory floor.

— H. Ross Perot on life at General Motors in the late '80s

Sometimes, It Ain't Pretty Out There

If you've made it this far in the book, you're starting to buy in to what I've been saying (even if just a bit), and you're starting to get a sense of excitement about creating a more humane, inspiring way to lead.

But I'm sure you've been asking yourself if this is all something out of Fantasyland. "Can this really work in the real world?"

The short answer – sure. But you're going to have to want it and you're going to have to work at it.

There are reasons, lots of them, as to why the state of leadership in general is so bad:

- The rise of "shareholder value"
- Downsizing/Outsourcing
- Globalization

All of which have contributed to an extremely short-term time-frame for any results. In this short-term world, employees have been used time and again to, in effect, "balance the books" by getting laid off by the hundreds, sometimes thousands. It has become an easy management "crutch" to prop up earnings, and Wall Street has contributed by rewarding this behavior. Very often the day after a company announces a round of layoffs the stock price will jump up. If the CEO plays the game right and does this near the end of a quarter, the stock price increase will allow the CEO to "make the numbers" and she'll get her bonus, these days running into the millions of dollars. In this kind of environment, why wouldn't the CEO want to try this again next quarter? (I over-dra-matize - but only a bit).

Because of this, in many organizations we're seeing the following characteristics among the employees: fear and insecurity (as people are afraid for their jobs); cynicism (people no longer believe the boss is always right; more important, they aren't sure management is acting in the best interests of the company); distrust (employees have learned not to trust); self-interest (people are realizing that their most important job is looking out for number one); confusion (employees everywhere are suffering from a deep—seated confusion about what is expected of them and what their role in the company will be); anomie (getting by at a job has replaced work that makes a real difference); and fragmentation (today there is little glue to bond people in a common quest).[1]

Does any of this sound familiar? I'm sure it does. These conditions are very, very pervasive across the business landscape these days. Does it depress you? It should; what our institutions have done, and are doing, to those of us who inhabit their hallways is unconscionable. More to the point, the pursuit of the short-term buck (okay, short-term millions of bucks) is hollowing out our businesses, killing productivity, and straining the social fabric to the point that it threatens our ability to compete.

Now, the $64,000 question: does all this scare you, or at the very least, make you wonder what you've signed up for? How in heaven's name, you may be asking, can I motivate a team if they feel like THAT?

This is your "bit of cold water". This in many places is what you're up against as a new leader. I don't want to be too much of a downer here, but I'd have been remiss if I'd only given you a book full of happy talk and then sent you out there to get your head (and your enthusiasm, ambition, and energy) chewed off. It's a cynical world out there, by and large, and it can be incredibly difficult to motivate people. Most managers (i.e., NOT leaders) don't even bother to try, either because they don't know how or because they themselves have settled into just looking out for #1.

And therein, my friends, lays (oddly enough) the nugget of the answer.

Here we go; hang with me:

- Just because this bad situation is pervasive doesn't mean we can't change it.
- Don't try to solve all the problems of the business world in your first ninety days.
- With so many managers "checked out" themselves, ANY leader who shows even the SMALLEST inkling that they not only sincerely care about doing a good job, they also actually care about their team will be an amazing change to the team. Just give a damn, and you'll make a big impression. They'll take notice.
- In some places it's so bad that all you have to do is follow through with the suggestions in this book, nail even most of the 10 for 90, and you'll have a reputation as a great boss in a very short period of time.
- The word will get out; people will want to work for you.
- Continue to build a little "oasis" of humane, rockin' leadership. Promote those who "get it"; perpetuate the movement!

If we're going to bring back leadership that celebrates and derives its power from people, I want you to be ready. I need you to be ready. One last reminder...

Stick Close to Your "Why"

We've talked about "the split" already, and how it can take you and your team away from their "why" and make you a victim of your own success.

Don't lose the power of your "why" or your team's "why". Avoid the split by constantly reaffirming the central place and central importance of the "why".

Never compromise on your "why". Ever. It protects you, by keeping you focused on ideals and goals that have the greater good, a higher reason, and away from the down-and-dirty world of office politics. You can't really completely avoid politics, but it has been my experience over twenty-five years that the political players ALWAYS get found out, ALWAYS lose. I'm not naïve here; sometimes political animals can go on a run that can last for years and make you wonder if anyone upstairs is paying attention. But over time, they WILL get found out and dealt with.

Your "why" is your power. Don't ever forget that either. It is the fuel that makes everything work.

The last and most important reason to stick close to your "why" and feed it daily -- the person/team with the most compelling "why" has the strongest convictions for what they're doing, where they're going, and how they're going to get there. Strong convictions give everyone a certainty that's nearly unstoppable.

"Why" gives people a reason to follow you; it's what inspires. Followers give you numbers, and in numbers there is strength and the capability to make change.

Recap & T.T.R.

- In the last twenty years, especially in the U.S., a short-term environment has developed that has gotten very, very unfriendly to people. It's nasty out there.
- Stand the nastiness on its head; use the fact that it's so bad out there in some places that it's very easy to stand out in a strong way.
- Be genuine; pay attention to your people; just give a damn.
- You can't fix it all; fix your little corner of the world. Promote those that "get it".
- Never EVER compromise your "why"; keep it close and well-fed.

Chapter Notes

[1]Terrence E. Dela and Alan A. Kennedy, *The New Corporate Cultures*, Perseus Publishing, 1999. Chapter 8.

CHAPTER 9

FINAL THOUGHTS

I love it when a plan comes together.

— *Col. Hannibal Smith, The A-Team*

Congratulations! You've made it to this final chapter! We've covered a lot of ground in a short time but hopefully you've been able to grab onto some hints, tips, and practical, actionable concepts that will help you make a serious impact and inspire your new team and anyone else working for you throughout your career.

In this final chapter, we'll cover some miscellaneous final thoughts that didn't really fit neatly in any of the other chapters but are valuable nonetheless.

Never Lose Sight of How Important You Are

You are, by definition, a "first-line" leader. That is, you have people directly reporting to you. You may not yet completely buy in to the change-the-world mantra I've been laying on you, so let me clue you in to one more powerful piece of leverage you have that can help you do exactly that. Study after study has shown conclusively that first-line leaders significantly influence the people that report to them.

First, you have the power to keep people gladly coming to work every day or wanting to leave. Many studies of employee exit interviews (that is, interviews done by HR with people who are leaving the company) contain a strong thread: the employees decided to leave because they didn't think anybody cared. They didn't feel appreciated at best and ignored at worst. The quite-natural thought process in those leaving was, "Well, if they don't care about me, why should I care about them? I'll go get a job somewhere where they notice an appreciate me." You'd think pay, or benefits, or working conditions might top the list; instead it's **the simple act of human kindness known as paying attention**, valuing someone as a person. Again, all the management theory goes out the window in lieu of the most basic human need of being noticed, being valued. As a first-line leader, you have the best opportunity of anyone in the organization to give your teammates what they need. It's SO easy. It's SO powerful.

Second, you're the one they see every day. As a first-line leader you are, whether you like it or not, the embodiment of "corporate management". Yes, they know there's a CEO, that there's a Divisional VP somewhere, but they may never ever see them. To a great extent, these people are mere concepts, or that sharply-dressed lady in the quarterly videos on the company's intranet. Your teammates will gauge what they feel about *all of management as well as the company* by how YOU act, how YOU treat people, how YOU respect others, and how YOU interact. This as you can figure will dovetail directly with the first point above; you color a tremendous portion of how your teammates feel about the whole organization and whether or not it's an ethical place that is worth them spending their time in.

If you didn't believe "people first" REALLY mattered before, now would be a great time to latch onto it and keep it close.

Shut Your Pie Hole!

An alternative title for this section could be Hey, Stupid, Just Listen! Another of the most basic of human needs is to be heard, to have our opinions valued. There have been at least a gazillion books written about listening and listening skills written over the years, all pointing to the importance of good listening. There's something about becoming a manager – I didn't say "leader" on purpose – though, that apparently makes nearly everyone close their ears and open their mouths. Perhaps it's the feeling of power, that the manager has the title and therefore by definition the manager's opinions are more important than the staff's. Or maybe it's ego. I'm not a psychologist.

Tom Peters, who we've met up with before, has an almost incredible statistic that he shares in some of his seminars. A study was done of physicians and THEIR listening habits. Now, as a physician, you would think that listening would be elevated to a SERIOUS art; after all, with all the variability of symptoms, reactions, and manifestations from person to person. You would think that as a physician, you would be keenly aware that the absolute best source of information about "what ails 'em" would be the patient themselves. With some intelligently placed questions, you would be able to draw out a detailed picture of what was bothering them, where the symptoms were targeted, how frequent and how severe they occurred, and any other noteworthy information.

And in fact this is exactly what physicians are taught, all through medical school and their internships.

What the study looked at was the time a physician remained quiet to listen to the patient describe their issue before beginning to speak. That is the time between when the physician said the usual "What seems to be the problem?" question and when they resumed talking.

After all their training, after years of learning how valuable the patient's own description of their problem is, how long do you think they give the patient, on average, before interrupting them?

18 SECONDS.

Really. No joke.[1]

Think how much better diagnoses could be if your friendly neighborhood Doc would just keep quiet.

Remember that you as a leader are relying on your people to get something done. Listening in the workplace too can provide invaluable tactical and problem-solving insight, and as I said earlier in this chapter it can make your team feel valued, important, and can keep them inspired and working for you way beyond what's necessary to keep their job (remember Discretionary Effort?)

Your team has great insights, perspectives, and troubleshooting ideas just to name a few. It can be yours just for the asking. And then shut the hell up.

Meetings Good vs. Meetings Bad

Meetings are one of those lightning-rod items that can start a conversation around the water-cooler faster than anything. And they quickly end up being a "can you top this?" contest where everyone pulls out their most annoying, bizarre, and just plain dreadful meetings they had to endure. I've participated in a few; it's always amazing how many brutal meetings there have been out there!

I'm here to tell you though, that meetings can not only be good, they can be great. Surprised?

Meetings, done well, do a number of things:

- Allow everyone hear the same message at the same time in a way that is more powerful than email.
- Allow the meeting organizer have a chance to gauge the reaction to whatever's being discussed.
- If the group is familiar with each other or is small, it is a great forum for dissent and debate.
- Allows you to get alignment on an upcoming decision or direction.
- Provide a chance for some social connection-building and networking.

But the REAL reason meetings are good, and why you should love them, is that they are your #1 leadership opportunity. Think of it: you've got everyone there either in the conference room or on the phone, and they are a captive audience, with a much more limited chance of interruption. In the course of a specific meeting timeframe you can transact some kind of work (the usual, frankly unimaginative approach), you can celebrate team/project milestones or other victories, you can drive home your vision, you can invite feedback to see how your message is being received, you can go over day-to-day situations that give you a chance to lay out and reinforce your values, and you can reinforce and remind everyone of the team's "why". In effect, you are "in performance" and showing them, once again, why and how you are a LEADER, not a manager. It is your stage, your "bully pulpit". Don't miss out on one of the best perks of being a leader; never look at a meeting as "just another meeting" again.

...

Bad meetings are a dime a dozen, unfortunately, so I won't go into too many of the gory details you likely already know. But I do have a few pet peeves that you should make sure NEVER happen during one of yours:

- Meetings that start late or run over.
  - These are the WORST. What the organizer is telling everyone is that they don't care at all about anybody's schedule but their own. If the meeting just can't be finished in the allotted time, schedule another meeting to finish up.
  - EXCEPTION: If you're about to run over, ask the attendees if they think the meeting can be wrapped up shortly (in no more than fifteen minutes). If everyone is okay with plugging along now to wrap things up, go for it.
- Someone joins late and the meeting organizer stops everything to give Mr. Tardy a recap of all that's gone on so far. Not only is this rude to everyone who DID show up on time, it is enabling Mr. Tardy! He'll think nothing of coming late to this organizer's next meeting, because he figures he'll be obliged with an update again next time. Please, upon pain of death, promise that you'll never do this.
- Not having a clear agenda for the meeting. It doesn't necessarily have to be written down, but know exactly what you

want as a result of every meeting you run. Without that the odds of this meeting becoming a colossal waste of time go WAY up.

- People who take calls or work their smartphones during the meeting should not be tolerated. If that person is your boss, you'll have to be a little more delicate. But it's rude and annoys almost everyone who has to watch it.
- Meetings with way too many attendees for the task at hand. Big meeting invariably limit dissent and debate, and the tendency toward "groupthink" goes way up. Don't over-invite.
- Meetings over an hour and a half long. I've NEVER seen a meeting longer than this that was productive. First, it's a big pain to schedule, and people don't like to commit such a big chunk of their day to one (likely boring and unproductive) meeting. The minute the meeting goes over an hour people will start to mentally drift as they start thinking of all the things they should be doing instead of sitting in this meeting. A friend of mine, a trainer by trade, said the first session he ever gave was over three hours long. In the student-evaluation surveys that came back after the session, one student observed, "The mind can only absorb what the seat can withstand." Don't ever forget that.

Priorities 101

Priorities are everywhere, no big surprise. Do this, then do that, then do the other thing. From the chairman of the board to your favorite cat, (eat first and then sleep or sleep first, **and then** eat?), priorities are the way of the world.

Funny thing is, most people don't know what their priorities are. Funnier yet, they will argue with you all day to convince you that they do. They will tell you, in an ever-louder voice that "X" is their number one priority, "Y" is most assuredly number two, and "Z" is definitely number three. If the person you're asking is an executive, they're used to playing this game and will likely stop at three. Other people, maybe wanting to appear more ambitious or more important may give you six or seven "top" priorities. And they will believe in their heart of hearts that they are telling you the truth. More than likely they're not.

You want to know what your (or anybody else's) real priorities are? Check your/their calendar. Because what we DO, from hour to hour, day to day, ARE our priorities, no matter what we might tell ourselves or others.

As an experiment, print out your Outlook or Notes calendar from the past month. Alternatively, keep a time log for a week noting what you do and when. Either way, take the printout/log and group the time into categories, such as "email", "forming strategy", "client contact", or whatever categories apply to you and your job. Then match it up against what you've been telling everyone your priorities are.

How do you measure up? If for example your "stated priority" is keeping close to the customer, how many hours per day/week do you spend "close to the customer"? If you're honest with yourself and you categorization your calendar is monopolized by a variety of mundane and largely unimportant tasks that have nothing whatsoever to do with "staying close to the customer": answering emails, checking your smartphone for the latest weather forecast, talking to the guy in the cubicle behind you about the latest charity drive at work, reformatting that status report for the third time… you get the point.

As you're checking what your "daily priorities" are, also take a look at what KIND of time your daily tasks are falling into. See the four-quadrant box below. If you graph out the typical distribution of work by putting an "X" in each quadrant for each hour spent, you'll get an accurate picture of what general categories your time is falling into:

	High Urgency	
Quadrant 2: Urgent, Not Important		**Quadrant 3:** Urgent, Important
Quadrant 1: Not Urgent, Not Important		**Quadrant 4:** Not Urgent, Important
	Low	

Low   *Importance*   High

Unless you're very, very disciplined already, the bulk of your time on a daily basis is likely spent in quadrants 1 and 2. Let's face it: left to their own accord, we end up doing a lot of non-important work, from answering emails (quadrant 1) and the "I gotta have that twelve-page report on my desk by 5 p.m.!" (Quadrant 2). Without being extremely diligent, it's too easy to get caught up in those two quadrants.

The priorities we typically give someone live, for the most part, in quadrants 3 and 4. Interestingly, we don't spend a lot of time in quadrant 3, primarily because this is either a crisis, fire drill, or the culmination of some event that spent a long time in quadrant 4.

As a leader especially, the most productive thing you can do is to hang out as much as you can in quadrant 4. This is the place where long-term, strategic tasks live. That three-year plan to revamp your accounting system? Working on it today is certainly not urgent, but oh-so-important. The real problem is that if you don't get to that three-year plan today because of some gotta-have-it item, it doesn't feel like a big deal at all. But too many days where it gets put off and now your three-year plan takes four years to accomplish.

To sum up, take a close look at your calendar to see what your day-to-day priorities are. See how that pays with what you think your priorities SHOULD be, and make changes. It will take a concerted focus to keep yourself from languishing too long in quadrants 1 or 2.

Recap & T.T.R.

- You as a first-line manager are incredibly important to how your people feel about the company and management. You can make a HUGE difference in the lives and careers of your team.
- Listen first. Speak later. And give it more than 18 seconds.
- Meetings can be fun, productive and a day-by-day opportunity to show your leadership. Take the stage and use it well!
- Focus on making your calendar match your priorities.

Chapter Notes

[1]Tom Peters video, "Leadership Thoughts: Listening", http://www.youtube.com/watch?v=IwB7NAvKPeo

NOW IT'S YOUR TIME

Time to turn you loose.

I've thrown a lot at you in a short amount of time; a distillation of the most important skills and concepts I've developed while building, re-building, and optimizing teams. My deepest hope is that you have found some things to latch onto, some things you can use now and in the future, to propel you to a great career as a leader, racking up a string of ever-more important accomplishments.

I ask but one thing: that you take these concepts to heart and resolve to become a people-centric, potential-developing leader.

I wrote this book because I have been saddened and angered by the utter destruction the last twenty years of short-sighted, profit at all cost, worker-as-bargaining-chip management has wrought. My goal is to start a movement; a new generation of leaders that remember how powerful a team of committed people are that trust each other, support each other, and move mountains along the way.

I've done what I wanted to do; plant a seed. What happens with that seed is up to you and what you do with it. The road may not always be smooth, but I urge you to stick with it and persevere. If you do, you will mold lives, change attitudes, and find potential in people that even they didn't know they had. And they (and you) will achieve more than you thought possible, creating a team that will resonate in your collective memories for years to come.

It is the greatest calling in the world, and now it's yours.

JUMP START!

...

As stated earlier, Jump Start! is only the beginning of the **High Voltage Leadership** method. If you want to take your newfound knowledge to the next level with additional training and insights, please join us at www.RedstoneServicesLLC.us to learn more.

Over time, I intend this to be a place where you (and leaders like you) can come to meet, be re-inspired, communicate ideas, and gain new skills to keep you at the top of your game. I want it to be your forum, your laboratory, your community. I want it to be your site; if you have a need, or an idea, either make a comment on the site.

Go there now to continue what you've started!

...

"Never doubt that a small group of committed people can change the world. Indeed it is the only thing that ever has."

— Margaret Mead

www.ingramcontent.com/pod-product-compliance
Lightning Source LLC
Chambersburg PA
CBHW051317170526
45166CB00002B/580